Garden ALMANAC

A MONTH-BY-MONTH GUIDE

BY

PENELOPE O'SULLIVAN

A FAIR STREET BOOK

Country Living
GARDENER

HEARST BOOKS
NEW YORK

Produced by Fair Street Productions
Project Director: Susan Wechsler
Editor: Barbara Ellis
Designer: Robert Bull Design
Copyeditor: Alexa Barre
Photo Research: Deborah Anderson/Photosearch, Inc.
Art Coordinators: Shaie Dively, Sandra Cullen
Consultant: Ruth Rogers Clausen/Horticulture Editor, *Country Living Gardener*
Production: Welcome Enterprises, Inc.

Library of Congress Cataloging-in-Publication Data

O'Sullivan, Penelope.
    A garden almanac : a month-by-month guide / by Penelope O'Sullivan and the editors of Country living gardener.
       p. cm.
    Includes index.
    ISBN 0-688-16619-9
    1. Gardening. 2. Almanacs, American. I. Country living gardener. II. Title
SB453.008 2000
635—dc21   99-37598
                                                  CIP

Printed in Singapore

First Edition

1 2 3 4 5 6 7 8 9 10

A Fair Street Book

www.williammorrow.com
www.cl-gardener.com

Table of Contents

Foreword

If you're anything like me, gardening is a passion that sometimes borders on obsession. Did I plant out those seedlings at just the right moment? Have the roses been pruned on time? Do I need to rotate my plots this spring? These sorts of questions continue to nag at me all through the year. Even in a bimonthly gardening magazine, we can't possibly address all the tasks that need to be accomplished. This is why we decided it would be a great idea to pull all the essential information a gardener needs into an almanac that can be referred to year in and year out. Every gardener, whether master or novice, can use a guide to seasonal garden tasks. *Garden Almanac: A Month-by-Month Guide* truly fills the bill; more experienced green thumbs may use it as a handy reminder, while people just beginning to garden will find this compendium of tips, tasks, and timetables indispensable.

In planning the book, a great deal of time was spent thinking about all the things we, as gardeners and avid garden book readers, would ideally like to have in an almanac; topping our "wish list" was concise information on what to do and when to do it, available right at our fingertips. Thus, the book is set up in a month-by-month format, so it's easy to find just what you're looking for. Tasks have been boxed off and bulleted, broken down into specific categories such as *Trees and Shrubs, Flowers and Grasses,* and *Fruits and Vegetables,* so you can navigate right to the information you need.

Every garden contains a variety of growing conditions, with each corner presenting a new challenge. Also, we all have different interests—whether it be attracting butterflies, growing cut flowers, or cultivating a potager so that we can relish the exceptional flavor of homegrown produce. Peppered throughout this guide are detailed descriptions sure to address your own special gardening interests or site considerations. In the flower bed surrounding my own front porch, I planted more than a thousand spring-flowering bulbs last fall. When the blooms faded I found the advice in *Bulb Care 101* on page 49 invaluable as I waited for the perennials to fill in around the ripening bulb foliage. My husband recently pulled up a long section of grass along the driveway to make way for a rose bed, so I immediately turned to a special feature, *Planting Bare-Root Roses,* on page 47, which explained exactly how to proceed.

At *Country Living Gardener,* we are dedicated to bringing you the best, most useful and relevant information possible, put together in a fun, easy-to-read format. I hope you find this terrific guide as helpful as I do. Happy Gardening!

— Diana Gold Murphy
Editor-in-Chief
Country Living Gardener

Introduction

This was one of my prayers: for a parcel of land not so very large, which should have a garden and a spring of ever-flowing water near the house, and a bit of woodland as well as these.

The Roman poet Horace (c. 65 B.C.E.) thus expressed his craving for nature's beauty and for the simple life—a pastoral longing familiar to many modern citizens, be they suburbanites, city dwellers, or people safely ensconced in the rural landscape. Gardening connects the soul to the earth, and it's fun—a way to wind down from daily stresses and enjoy the pleasure of creating something both useful and beautiful. Gardens, like life, are stories of growth and change, of works in progress, of continuity in cycles. Many of my plants are gifts from gardening friends generous with seeds, cuttings, and divisions of their favorite varieties. In turn, when I divide a perennial, harvest herbs, or collect seeds, I share the wealth with my friends and neighbors.

Garden Almanac offers informative tips, garden advice, horticultural information, and a substantial chronological list of activities to help keep your garden beautiful and flourishing throughout the year, no matter what the level of your aspirations. Gardening novices will find the almanac useful as a learning tool; experienced gardeners will refer to the tasks as helpful reminders, and relish, perhaps, some new-found tips. This wealth of information is divided for easy access into four basic categories: *The Whole Garden, Trees & Shrubs, Flowers & Grasses,* and *Fruits & Vegetables.*

Though weather and location affect a gardener's timing of specific chores, there's still a universal rhythm to the gardener's year, a waxing and waning of activities indoors and out. In my garden, spring means mud. Summer is perfect—a succession of long, sunny days with cerulean skies. Breathtakingly clear autumns and seemingly endless, cold, gray-and-white winters complete the seasonal cycle.

I live in Zone 5 on Great Bay, an estuary of the Atlantic Ocean in New Hampshire, but most of the plants mentioned in this book are hardy in USDA Zones 3-6. Think carefully not only about the climate of your region, but about the microclimate of your own garden. For example, I can grow Zone 6 plants in a garden bed against the sunny south side of my house. The bed enjoys a double helping of warmth and sunshine; no trees obstruct the sunlight, which then is reflected back again off the pale yellow clapboards of my house.

I've written this book from the perspective of my particular latitude and longitude, but its timing can be adjusted to suit your zone. In colder climates, you'll need to perform many of the outdoor tasks a couple of weeks earlier in the fall, since the ground will freeze sooner. In warmer areas, you can take care of spring tasks earlier in the year and fall tasks later. Similarly, a cold spring can delay the performance of many tasks, while a particularly warm spring may speed them up.

The last frost date in spring and the first frost date in autumn determine the length of your growing season;

the dates for your area, along with other gardening information, are available from your local Cooperative Extension Service. Established in 1914, the Cooperative Extension system is a public partnership between the United States Department of Agriculture and the land-grant universities authorized in 1862 and 1890. Part of the Extension's mission is to educate the public through research-based knowledge of agriculture and home economics. Local Extension agents are gold mines of information on horticulture in specific areas of the country.

Each chapter of this monthly almanac is illustrated with a flower arrangement from *Twelve Months of Flowers*, a seed catalogue and gardening book written by Robert Furber in 1730. Furber, an English nurseryman, used these botanically correct copper engravings to sell his plant materials; they were indexed with numbers and names to make studying the plates and placing orders more convenient. Although some of his plants may be unfamiliar to you, or may not be hardy in your garden, they offer a fascinating, aesthetically pleasing glimpse into garden history. Each month, we use these plates to inspire ideas for creating contemporary bouquets from your garden and florist shop.

Just as the cycles of various plants fluctuate throughout the year, so too do the cycles of various members of the animal kingdom. The more I garden, the more I see how plants, insects, birds, fish, animals, and humans interact in nature. In the garden, flora and fauna blend their rhythms and unite in a joyful whole. Bluebirds arrive in March, Japanese beetles by July, and monarch butterflies thrill me at summer's end. Welcoming—even inviting—some wildlife into your garden can dramatically enrich the gardening experience; accordingly, I have included some pertinent observations in this almanac.

Gardening is not only a science, it is an art. Each garden, and each gardener, is unique. Whether it's weeding, vegetable cultivation, or growing and arranging flowers, do the tasks you enjoy, work on those that enhance the areas of the garden that are important to you. If one day you find yourself in the garden, eager to work but with nothing to do, consult these pages for ideas. And if your job keeps you too busy to garden—don't despair! The garden will wait for you. You may need to change your plans by, for example, purchasing starter plants instead of growing plants from seed, but you will still enjoy a garden of beauty and delight.

Much of the advice and information in this book has been drawn from my experience as a home gardener, a garden writer, and a master gardener with the Rockingham County, New Hampshire, Cooperative Extension, where I was privy to the common and uncommon questions and concerns of new gardeners. May you learn from and adapt to your own use these trials and tribulations, experiments that have succeeded or failed, problems encountered and solved, and most of all, the love and pleasure of gardening.

Acknowledgments

Many knowing and talented people helped me write this book. Some who encouraged or advised me include: Vicki Duguay at Johnny's Selected Seeds in Albion, Maine; Nancy Adams and Nada Hadda of the Rockingham County, New Hampshire, Cooperative Extension; Dennis Hayward of Bio-Spray in Greenland, New Hampshire (who knows pest control inside and out); Barbara Ellis, my editor, whose discernment and knowledge I trust; Bob Bull, whose extraordinary page designs make my words sing; Susan Wechsler of Fair Street Productions, whose vision, perseverance, and discriminating taste made this entire project possible; and Betty Rice of Hearst Books as well as the editors at *Country Living Gardener* magazine, who enthusiastically supported this book. Finally, to Bob, Nick, and Molly, who push me ever onward: You're the best.

The producers acknowledge the institutions who provided us with information, illustrations, and support, and especially thank the following individuals: Renee Beaulieu/White Flower Farms; Tony Constanzo/The Clark Foundation, Cooperstown, NY; Linda Detrick; Laurie Eichengreen/Greensense; Susan Frei/Ursus Books; Dency Kane; Michael Melford; Jerry Pavia; Jim White; The Hunt Institute of Botanical Documentation.

Picture Credits

Courtesy, Agricultural Research Service, United States Department of Agriculture: 176; Christie's Images, NY: 49, 82; Courtesy, Tony Costanzo, The Clark Foundation, Cooperstown, NY: 60, 61, 97, 167, 168, 169; Rosalind Creasy: 103, 117, 119, 135; Alan and Linda Detrick: 18, 21, 24, 31, 37, 46, 50, 53, 67, 78, 79, 83(left), 91, 92, 96, 99, 106, 108, 114, 131, 156, 159, 160 ; Fair Street Pictures: 26, 27, 52, 62, 80, 100, 121, 174; Flora Graphics: 22, 95, 98, 102, 110, 118, 132, 133, 136(left), 137, 147,161; Courtesy, Goldsmith Seeds, Inc.: 30, 172; Claudia Goldstein: 35; Dency Kane: 35, 39, 45, 59, 64, 65, 74, 76, 83(right), 112, 113, 151,158; The Library of Congress: 170, 111; Courtesy, Longwood Gardens, Kennett Square, PA; Photo by Larry Albee: 148; Charles Mann: 84; Michael Melford: 2, 20, 94, 125, 144; Jerry Pavia: 12, 15, 51, 75, 138, 143, 146, 149, 163, "Fruits & Vegetables" border, "Whole Garden" border; Max Polster Archive: 14; Private Collection: 90; The Singer logo is a registered trademark of Singer Company, Limited: 156, 174; Ursus Books, NY: 25, 38, 47, 66, 71, 77, 88, 101, 134; VIREO: W. Green 11, B. Henry 19, S. Fried 175; White Flower Farm, Litchfield, CT: 34, 40, 62, 70, 128.

From *Diderot Pictorial Encyclopedia of Trades and Industry*, 1751–52, Dover Publications, Inc.: 120,155; From *Dissertation Sur La Génération et Les Transformations des Insectes . . .* by Maria Sibylla Merian, 1726. Rare Books Division, The New Public Library, Astor, Lenox & Tilden Foundations: 36; From *The Flower Garden: Its Cultivation, Arrangement and General Management* by McIntosh, 19th century. Private Collection: 7, 63, 109; From *The Flower Grower's Guide*, Virtue and Company, 19th century. Private Collection: 13, 23, 34, 93, 126; From *Histoire des Arbres Forestiers de l'Amerique Septentrionale* by Francois-André Michaux, 1810–13. The Library of Congress: 9, 157; From *Hortus Eystettensis, Norimberque, Quintus Ordo*, Fol. 1, Vol. 1 by Basil Besler, 1613. Print Collection, Miriam and Ira D. Wallach Division of Art, Prints and Photographs. The New Public Library, Astor, Lenox & Tilden Foundations: 116; From *Hortus Floridus* by Crispijn van de Passe, 1614–16. The Library of Congress: 58; From *A New Orchard Garden: or, The Best Way for Planting, Grafting* by William Lawson, 1660. The Library of Congress: 44; From *Our Woodlands, Heaths & Hedges. A Popular Description of Trees, Shrubs, Wild Fruits . . .* by S. Coleman, 19th century. Private Collection: Cover, 103, 127, 150; From *Pomona Britannica* by George Brookshaw, 1804–12. The Library of Congress: 81, 173; From *The Quadrupeds of North America* by John James Audubon, 1856. The Library of Congress: 57, 72; From *Twelve Months of Flowers* by Robert Furber, 1730. Courtesy of Hunt Institute of Botanical Documentation, Carnegie Mellon University, Pittsburgh, PA: 5, 17, 29, 43, 55, 68, 87, 105, 123, 141, 153, 165.

Winter

... Crow gangs caw and scream in barren trees, scavenge on snow-covered lawn. Gravid gray sky says more snow. Miscanthus, which sparkles in sunlight, droops today.

JANUARY'S TASKS

THE WHOLE GARDEN

- Collect seed and plant catalogues.
- Check the dates on seed packets that you already own.
- Read your catalogues thoroughly before ordering new seeds or plants.
- Read gardening books for inspiration and new approaches to your landscape.
- Study the bare bones of your garden and make notes on potential improvements.
- Tour your garden to look for plant damage.
- Plan new gardens.
- Place your seed orders.
- Beware of a January thaw!
- Apply winter mulch.

TREES AND SHRUBS

- Remove excess snow from shrubs, especially those planted close to the roofline of the house.
- Use Christmas trees and holiday greens to protect plants from frost heave.
- Prune dead or broken branches off trees.
- Prune summer- and fall-blooming woody vines and shrubs while they are dormant.
- Fertilize acid-loving shrubs, if you didn't fertilize them in the fall.
- If you forgot to apply antidesiccant to your broad-leaved evergreens in late fall, do it now.
- Water broad-leaved and needled evergreens during a thaw.

FLOWERS AND GRASSES

- Routinely inspect houseplants and outdoor plants overwintered indoors for pests and diseases.
- Water indoor plants less frequently until they return to active growth.
- Pinch and turn houseplants to keep them shapely.
- Keep houseplants clean.
- Avoid excessive salt use on icy paths and driveways.

FRUITS AND VEGETABLES

- Make a plan to rotate vegetable crops when designing next year's garden.
- Prune fruit trees now that they are dormant.

Janu

Midwinter bouquets have a stark beauty uniquely their own. The Furber engraving at right shows January flowers in muted red, gold, and silver. In my New Hampshire bouquet, the colors are even bleaker—wintry tan and silvery blue-green. For me, bouquet making is a cross between meditation and fun, an excuse to pull on my boots, escape the computer, and explore outdoors. From my garden comes *Miscanthus sinensis*, an ornamental grass with elegant tan plumes and long dried curling leaves. In a marsh, I find the grass *Phragmites*, its puffy tan flowers looking ravaged and blowsy and its tan papery leaves tilting like lances in every direction. I stick them in a jug with dried milkweed pods and eastern white pine twigs and cones. The fine-textured blue-green needles add softness and a touch of color to the arrangement. Minimal in feeling, this arrangement has a welcome austerity following the sensory overload of the holidays.

Look around the garden for a bent twig, a fat seedpod, and some evergreen sprigs. If your garden lacks material for a January bouquet, add some plants with winter interest to your want-to-grow list. In addition to ornamental grasses, try conifers ranging in color from true gold and icy blue to blackish green, and broad-leaved evergreens with yellow, pink, or white variegation. Include shrubs and trees with red, yellow, or lime green stems or with abundant, persistent fruit in red, yellow, orange, and black. The berries will please you with their looks and supply a much needed food source for the birds.

1 Pellitory with daisy flowers.
2 Winter Aconite.
3 Great early Snow drop.
4 Single Snow drop.
5 White edged Polyanthos.
6 Dou.ble Peach colou.d Hepatica.
7 Double blew Violet.
8 Winter blew Hyacinth.
9 Lesser black Hellebor.
10 Dwarf white King Spear.
11 Ilex leav'd Jasmine.
12 Red Spring Cyclamen.
13 Acacia or sweet button tree.
14 White Cyclamen.
15 Creeping Borage or Buglofs.
16 Strip'd Spurge.
17 Lisbon Lemmon tree.
18 Canary Campanula.
19 Dwarf Tithymall.
20 Double Stock.
21 Filbert tree in flower.
22 True Venetian Vetch.
23 Seville Orange.
24 Grey Aloe.
25 Winter white Hyacinth.
26 Spotted Aloe.
27 Narrow curl'd leav'd Bay.
28 Tree Savory.
29 Triangle Yellow Ficoides.
30 Strip'd Orange.
31 Strip'd Candy tuft.
32 Tree Sedum.
33 Single blew Anemone.

JANUARY

From the Collection of Rob.t Furber gardener at Kensington 1730.

Designed by P.t Casteels.

Engrav'd by H. Fletcher.

What a relief to withdraw from the surfeit of holiday color and conviviality! Now we recover ourselves; we go back to the cave and dream about the garden to be. This is the gardener's month for study and introspection, because who we are and what we want affects what our garden will become. Plants grow in the imagination. Houseplants need care, and—I like this part the best—seed and plant catalogues arrive.

THE WHOLE GARDEN

- **Collect seed and plant catalogues** as they arrive and keep them together in a central location. (For me, it's a wingback chair in my husband's office, which is by the front door.) Your organization will pay off later. Too many times I have gotten excited about a particular plant, only to discover that I can't find the catalogue when I'm ready to order. Now, when I spot an enticing cultivar, I check it off, turn down the page, and toss the catalogue back on the pile until I'm ready to order.

- **Check the dates on seed packets that you already own.** Don't throw out last year's half-full seed packets; you may be able to use them again this year. Most seeds remain viable for three years, so it's worth holding on to the partially filled packets. After 3 years, germination is less successful. Check the expiration date on the packet if you're in doubt. By the way, if you collect your own seed, always write the collection date on the container.

- **Read your catalogues thoroughly before ordering new seeds or plants.** Catalogues make terrific winter reading for gardeners. They tell of new plant introductions that may help solve specific growing problems you've encountered, and are often the first place you can read about improvements in pest and disease resistance. Some seed companies gear their catalogues toward readability, with recipes, growing tips, and luscious descriptions that stimulate your imagination and turn your thoughts to garden design.

■ **Read gardening books for inspiration and new approaches to your landscape.** If you love reading books about English gardens and stately homes but know that you have neither the time, the patience, nor the climate for a Gertrude Jekyll border, think about a Jekyll-inspired plant or color combination in your backyard. Be adventurous and have fun!

Old garden books can be a great source of new ideas. Look for ways to scale back elaborate designs such as this one to fit the time and space you have available.

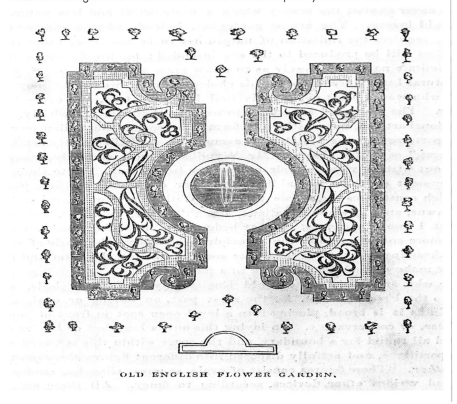

OLD ENGLISH FLOWER GARDEN.

■ **Study the bare bones of your garden and take notes on potential improvements.** One of winter's blessings is that it provides an opportunity to see your garden in a new light. The winter garden can be beautiful in its own right, particularly if its basic structure (the evergreens, deciduous trees and shrubs, and hardscape elements such as paths and fences) remains clear even under a foot of snow. See how you can improve your garden's structure and research plants to grow for seasonal interest next winter.

■ **Tour your garden to look for plant damage.** Walk carefully, keeping to mulched or paved paths where possible, since walking on frozen grass can harm your lawn. Winter plant damage includes branches broken by the weight of snow or ice and perennials or newly planted shrubs that have heaved from the ground during a cycle of freezing and thawing. Snip broken twigs ¼ inch from the branch with sharp pruners and press heaved plants back into the ground.

■ **Plan new gardens.** For gardeners, this is a wonderful time of year to recuperate from holiday bustle by dreaming about the season to come. Sink into a comfortable chair with colored pencils and paper. Close your eyes. Think about the plants you want to grow and the ideas you gleaned from your reading. Put your thoughts on paper with words and sketches.

■ **Place your seed orders.** Now that you know what you want to grow and where to grow it, order seeds before inventories run low. With seeds in hand, can sowing be far away?

■ **Beware of a January thaw!** Snow insulates the garden from temperature fluctuations, but during a January thaw the temperature warms up and the snow melts, leaving the ground bare and plants unprotected. A subsequent hard freeze can actually push shallow-rooted plants right out of the soil. Newly planted perennials, shrubs, and evergreens are particularly at risk.

■ **Apply winter mulch.** If severe temperatures are normal in your area, lay evergreen boughs or straw over vulnerable plants and garden beds for insulation when the ground freezes and before the January thaw.

TREES AND SHRUBS

■ **Remove excess snow from shrubs, especially those planted close to the roofline of the house.** Snow accumulating on a slanted roof can become so heavy that it slides off the surface in a mini-avalanche, crushing already snow-covered evergreens and breaking brittle branches on twiggy shrubs planted below. To prevent this calamity, gently brush the snow off the branches before it has a chance to harden. Let ice on trees and shrubs melt on its own. Chipping ice off branches or breaking icicles can do more damage than the ice itself. Think about building a wooden shelter over vulnerable shrubs next fall or transplanting them away from the roofline in spring or fall.

■ **Use Christmas trees and other holiday greens to protect plants from frost heave.** A live tree is an investment with benefits that can last all winter. Use cut boughs from the tree to cover plants and protect them from harsh weather. Or chip them up along with other holiday greens to use as mulch. Compost other natural decorations, but discard items coated with paint or any other synthetics in the trash.

- **Prune dead or broken branches off trees.** Ice and snow can break branches right off. Make clean cuts near the base of damaged branches, since jagged spots are entry points for pests and diseases.

- **Prune summer- and fall-blooming woody vines and shrubs while they are dormant.** On wisteria, for example, shorten the lateral shoots that you first cut back in July by about half.

- **Fertilize acid-loving shrubs, if you didn't fertilize them in the fall.** Hollies, leucothöe, rhododendrons, and azaleas benefit from an application of well-rotted manure or a 5-10-5 fertilizer.

- **If you forgot to apply antidesiccant to your broad-leaved evergreens in late fall, do it now;** it helps keep the leaves from drying out in harsh winter winds. Apply on a day when the temperature goes above 40°F.

- **Water broad-leaved and needled evergreens during a thaw.** When a spell of warm weather arrives in winter, these plants begin to transpire water through their leaves. Since water in the soil remains frozen, they are unable to replace lost moisture unless they are watered, and might suffer leaf scorch.

Balsam fir (*Abies balsamifera*).

Birds and Bees

SHRUBS FOR FALL AND WINTER BERRIES

For energy, birds depend on various food sources, including seeds, nectar, worms, insects, flowers, foliage, and berries. In spring and summer, when insects and nectar are plentiful, birds do gardeners a good turn by helping keep down populations of pests. In autumn and winter, however, bird food may be scarce. Encourage birds to overwinter and raise their families in your yard by planting shrubs that offer dense twigs for cover and nesting sites and long-lasting berries for winter food. Then, as soon as insects abound in spring, the birds will be on hand to eat them.

Gardeners can help birds find year-round sustenance by growing shrubs with fruit that matures at different times. Remember that many birds such as robins, bluebirds, and cedar waxwings are attracted to berry- or fruit-producing vines and shrubs. While hungry people salivate at the sight of a fast-food restaurant, hungry birds head straight for poison ivy and Virginia creeper. Birds also flock to many plants that are more appealing to gardeners, including bright red-fruited winterberries and viburnums. The different species of viburnum attract more than 30 species of birds, including cedar waxwings and rose-breasted grosbeaks. After the birds have digested their food, they excrete the seeds, ensuring their own survival and that of the ingested plant species.

The following shrubs not only provide, for northern gardens, a fabulous fall or winter display, they also bear fruit to sustain both migrating birds and your garden's year-round residents.

Red chokeberry (*Aronia arbutifolia*) is a spreading, pest-free native, hardy to Zone 5. 'Brilliantissima' has superior red fall color. Even after the leaves have dropped, it holds its bright red fruit on bare branches. The common name chokeberry derives from the sour taste of the berries, which birds will eat only after they've consumed everything else. Or, consider black chokeberry (*Aronia melanocarpa* var. *elata*), which is hardy to Zone 3. More than 20 bird species are known to eat chokeberries, including catbirds, flickers, bluebirds, and ruffed grouse.

Japanese barberry (*Berberis thunbergii*) bears fruit eaten by cedar waxwings from October well into winter. Birds like this thorny, densely branched shrub both for cover and for food, while people appreciate its vigor and striking fall color. Yellow-leaved cultivars include 'Aurea', which grows slowly up to 4 feet high, and red-fruited 'Bonanza Gold', which is 2 feet tall. Variegated forms exist, as do green cultivars like 'Vermilion' with superior fall color. Many people grow purple-leaved forms of the shrub, the most popular being the 2-foot tall *Berberis thunbergii* var. *atropurpurea* 'Crimson Pygmy'. Hardy to Zone 4.

Winterberry (*Ilex verticillata*), a deciduous holly that is hardy to Zone 3, makes a gorgeous show of color in late fall and early winter, until the deep cold darkens its brilliant red fruit. Outstanding cultivars of this Northeastern native include 'Fairfax', 'Tiasquam', and 'Winter Red'. The fruit of these cultivars, and of the spectacular hybrid 'Sparkleberry', may last through February or even longer. 'Aurantiaca' bears a lavish crop of orange fruits that do not persist as long as many red ones. Fruiting winterberries are female plants that require a nearby male blooming at the same time for fertilization. 'Southern Gentleman' is a good pollinator for both 'Winter Red' and 'Sparkleberry'. Winterberry attracts bluebirds, cedar waxwings, and brown thrashers.

Linden viburnum (*Viburnum dilatatum*), and several of its cultivars—including 'Oneida,' 'Catskill', and 'Iroquois—bear their bright red fruit from autumn into December. Hardy to Zone 4.

European cranberrybush viburnum (*Viburnum opulus*) has big round berries that turn vivid red in fall. The berries shrivel once freezing weather arrives and may stay on the shrub through winter. Hardy to Zone 3.

American cranberrybush viburnum (*Viburnum trilobum*) is a native with red fruits that not only delight cedar waxwings year after year, but also make delicious jams and jellies for human consumption. This viburnum may also bring ruffed grouse, rose-breasted grosbeaks, and bluebirds to your garden. Hardy to Zone 2.

Tea viburnum (*Viburnum setigerum*), hardy from Zones 5–7, is a fascinating plant. When mature, it stands bare-legged in the garden, its arching branches concentrated on the top two-thirds of the plant. Its unusual habit lends it an oriental grace that is accentuated in the fall, when bunches of intense orangey red fruit hang on the drooping branches.

Northern bayberry (*Myrica pensylvanica*) is a tough suckering shrub hardy to Zone 2. Native to the Northeast coast, bayberry tolerates salt, poor soil, and both wet or dry conditions. Depending on the location, it varies in height from 5 to 12 feet. Prolific, fragrant, waxy light gray berries on female plants look handsome after the leaves have dropped, and persist throughout the winter. Bluebirds, downy woodpeckers, and more than 80 other bird species may eat the berries.

Wintercreeper (*Euonymus fortunei*), hardy to Zone 4, is a popular evergreen climber and ground cover available with green, yellow, or variegated leaves. Ruddy fall fruits open to expose persistent orange-coated seeds that are appealing to birds. Wintercreeper tolerates deep shade and dry, poor soil. Bluebirds and robins enjoy the berries of several species of *Euonymus* .

Red osier dogwood (*Cornus sericea*) is native to wet places in the Northeast. Hardy to Zone 2, this spreading shrub has dark red winter bark that stands out in the landscape. The cultivar 'Flaviramea' is notable for its bright yellow winter bark. Like other dogwoods, this species produces fall fruit attractive to many birds. Siberian dogwood (*Cornus alba* 'Sibirica') is similar in habit and culture to red osier dogwood, but its stems are bright red. The cultivar 'Argenteo-marginata' has white-bordered leaves, making it an ornamental addition to the landscape every season of the year. Dogwood species provide food for more than 90 species of birds, including robins, flickers, bluebirds, and cardinals.

FLOWERS AND GRASSES

■ **Routinely inspect houseplants and outdoor plants overwintered indoors for pests and diseases.** Even if you carefully inspected houseplants and tender perennials before bringing them indoors in fall, check them routinely for problems throughout the winter. Look at the soil and the tops and bottoms of leaves. Feel the leaves. Stray aphids, mealy bugs, scale, or whiteflies can multiply quickly indoors and create serious, full-blown infestations by wintertime. Promptly isolate infested plants and treat them with insecticidal soap.

Keep cane-stemmed or angelwing begonias barely moist and cool (65° to 70°F) over winter. Repot and prune in spring.

■ **Water indoor plants less frequently until they return to active growth.** Like many living things, plants need winter rest. In winter, daylight hours decrease, plants go dormant or grow very slowly, and the need for water and nourishment diminishes. Plants that need weekly summer watering may require little water in winter —perhaps once every 2 to 3 weeks. To keep your plants comfortable, use tepid water.

■ **Pinch and turn houseplants to keep them shapely.** Pinching a plant's growing stem tips causes branching and bushy growth, as it diverts energy from stem ends into lateral buds. Since houseplants will grow toward the light, giving them a quarter-turn once a week also encourages shapely growth.

■ **Keep houseplants clean.** Dust and dirt affects a plant's absorption of life-giving sunlight, water, and carbon dioxide. To clean smooth-leaved plants, spray tepid water on them, or set them in the shower. If your houseplant has big leaves, you can also clean them with a damp cloth. Brush the dust off African violets and other hairy-leaved plants with a sable watercolor brush, since spraying water on the leaves of African violets causes brown spots.

■ **Avoid excessive salt use on icy paths and driveways.** Too much salt harms your lawn and borders, eventually killing the grass and flowers that it touches. Inexpensive fertilizer or wood ashes are good salt substitutes.

TIP Florist gloxinias (left) are rewarding but challenging houseplants. Give them 4 hours of bright, indirect light daily, or grow them under fluorescent lights. Keep them cool (60° to 70°F) and water when the top inch of soil is dry to the touch. Avoid wetting the leaves when watering. A pebble tray under the pot helps keep humidity high.

January

Damage Control

WHITEFLIES

With their habit of sticking close to their host plant, adult whiteflies are particularly irritating, extremely visible pests. Tap an infested houseplant and a ghostly horde flits off the leaves and hovers nearby. Whiteflies secrete sticky, shiny honeydew. Their green larvae, hatched from eggs on the undersides of leaves, suck plant sap, causing leaves to yellow and drop. A severe infestation can kill a plant.

The moment whiteflies decide to make a home on your houseplants, take corrective measures. If you catch the problem early, you can treat it by spraying the leaves—top and bottom—with tepid water. Pay particular attention to the undersides. If that doesn't work, spray insecticidal soap on the foliage. (Make your own soap spray with one-half teaspoon Ivory liquid to a quart of water.) If you still find whiteflies, try one of these plant-based, organic poisons: Neem spray is effective at killing whiteflies, yet only toxic to pets and people if ingested; Pyrethrin sprays are also effective but somewhat more toxic.

FRUITS AND VEGETABLES

■ **Make a plan to rotate vegetable crops when designing next year's garden.** Don't grow the same crops in the same spot 2 years in a row, since each vegetable family is vulnerable to distinct pests and diseases. Moreover, some crops consume far more nutrients in the soil than others—the hungriest vegetables include tomatoes, peppers, eggplant, and potatoes, and members of the cabbage family including broccoli, Brussels sprouts, cauliflower, kale, radishes, and turnips. Rotate these crops with legumes such as peas and beans or cover crops like alfalfa and clover, which benefit the soil. Wait 3 years before replanting a particular crop in the same place.

■ **Prune fruit trees now that they are dormant.** If your pear or apple trees have branches growing low on the trunk, cut them off. Correct crossed or rubbing branches or branches that grow directly above one another by removing the weaker branch.

Dormant apple trees, decorated by a winter's snowfall, wait for spring.

THE WHOLE GARDEN:

- There's still time to look through catalogues, and place orders.
- Order bulbs and plants for spring planting.
- Thoroughly clean any flats or pots for seedlings.
- Set aside a potting area for seed starting and gather the necessary equipment.
- Sow those seeds that will need 10 to 12 weeks indoors before they can be transplanted outside.
- Make sure your bluebird boxes are clean.
- Beware of a February thaw!
- Continue looking for plant damage in the garden.

TREES AND SHRUBS:

- Continue removing excess snow—not ice—from shrubs.
- Prune off broken twigs and branches on shrubs.
- Prune trees, except for birches, flowering cherries, maples, horse chestnuts, lindens, and walnuts.
- Cut stems of spring-flowering shrubs for forcing.

FLOWERS AND GRASSES:

- Bring potted bulbs inside for forcing so they will flower by Easter.
- Continue inspecting houseplants and outdoor plants overwintered indoors for pests and diseases.
- Continue keeping houseplants in topnotch shape by pinching, turning, and cleaning them.
- Water indoor plants sparingly—and avoid fertilizing them altogether—until you see signs of active growth.
- Wrap houseplants carefully if you have to take them outdoors.
- Propagate geraniums by cuttings for late-spring planting.
- Avoid excessive salt use on icy paths.

FRUITS AND VEGETABLES:

- Plan your vegetable seed-sowing strategy.
- Begin sowing leek seeds indoors.
- Prune fall-bearing raspberries in late February.

If you force bulbs and branches, you can create an 18th-century garden look, like the one in the Furber engraving. Or, why not fight the February blahs with dried flowers? They're easy to work with and bring subtle but welcome color to a room. Last summer I saved stems of 'Coronation Gold' yarrow from a vase of fresh flowers in my dining room. I trimmed the stems, which were topped with perfect, flat, golden flower heads, and placed them in a vase. Then I dismantled an old arrangement of peegee hydrangea blossoms, throwing out tatty ones and placing the others with the yarrow. The combination of cream- , rose- , and green-tinted hydrangeas enfolding mustard yellow yarrow now heightens the reddish cast of a mahogany desk. Don't be afraid to use what's on hand indoors or in the garden. The spiny centers of purple coneflowers and the rusty brown spikes of anise hyssop make dramatic accents in winter arrangements.

Now is the perfect time to plan bouquets to pick from the garden come summer. Consider ordering annuals such as cosmos and sunflowers for the cutting garden, and while you are poring over catalogues, why not add seeds for annuals that attract butterflies? Butterflies love cosmos (*Cosmos bipinnatus*) a 3- to 5-foot annual with red, white, pink, or lavender flowers from early summer to frost. They also adore 2- to 10-foot-tall sunflowers (*Helianthus annus*), which come in shades of yellow, orange, creamy white, or reddish brown. Sunflowers also provide food for butterfly larvae and seeds for birds. Other annuals that make great additions to butterfly gardens include flossflower (*Ageratum houstonianum*), marigolds (*Tagetes patula*), petunias (*Petunia × hybrid*a), bachelor's buttons (*Centaurea cyanus*), and zinnias (*Zinnia* spp.).

1 Duke Vantol Tulip.
2 Silver Edg.d Alaternus.
3 Yellow blotch Alaternus.
4 Cornelian Cherry.
5 White Mezereon.
6 Red Mezereon.
7 Double Narcissus of Constantinople.
8 Single Anemone Purple & White.
9 Venetian Vetch true.
10 Double blew Hepatica.
11 Early white Hyacinth.
12 Blush red Dens Caninus.
13 Spring Cyclamen white Edg.d
14 Strip.d & Edg.d Polyanthus.
15 Single white Hepatica.
16 Single blew Hepatica.
17 White Dens Caninus.
18 Double Peach colour'd Hepatica.
19 The greater Snow-drop.
20 White Crocus.
21 Double Snow-drop.
22 Small yellow Crocus.
23 Great blew Crocus.
24 Small blew Crocus.
25 Single dark-red Anemone.
26 Pantaloon Strip'd Polyanthos.
27 Persian Iris.
28 Yellow dutch Crocus.
29 Scotch white Strip'd Crocus.
30 Blew Hyacinth Passionate.
31 Great bearing Almond.
32 Great bearing Almond.
33 Single Persian blew Anemone.
34 Peach colour'd single Hepatica.
35 Double Pilewort.

FEBRUARY

From the Collection of Rob.t Furber Gardiner at Kensington 1752

Design'd by P.t Casteels.

Engrav'd by H.Flerches.

February marks the beginning of real dirty-hands gardening. The childhood satisfaction of playing in mud starts here, except now we deal with pre-bagged potting mixes instead. All our dreaming, note-taking, and organization pays off in the pleasure of *doing*. Starting seeds is a simple act of faith, an expectation that something valuable will grow from hidden specks in a fertile host. During a February thaw, my sap starts to flow. Even though, in reality, there are three more months of drab days and cold nights here up North, I start to believe that spring will come again.

THE WHOLE GARDEN

- **Order bulbs and plants for spring planting.** For the best selection, especially if you are ordering new or unusual perennials or bulbs, it is important to get orders in as early as possible.

- **Thoroughly clean any flats or pots for seedlings.** Cleanliness is important when it comes to starting seeds, since unwashed materials can harbor pests and diseases. Ideally, sterilize pots and flats in a 10 percent solution of bleach (one part bleach to 10 parts water).

- **Set aside a potting area for seed starting and gather the necessary equipment.** It's much easier to tackle starting seeds when you're well-organized and have everything you need right at hand. If you decide on a table or kitchen counter for your potting area, cover it with newspaper before you begin. In addition to a sterile seed-starting mix—2 parts peat moss to 1 part vermiculite or perlite works well—you need containers or trays in which seeds and seedlings can grow. An electric heating mat improves and speeds germination.

- **Sow those seeds that will need 10 to 12 weeks indoors before they can be transplanted outside.** Petunias, zonal geraniums, impatiens, and peppers are some popular plants that need to be started indoors early to produce good-sized plants by the last spring frost date.

- **Make sure your bluebird boxes are clean.** Wearing rubber gloves, throw out old nests, which can overwinter pests that harm the very birds you're trying to attract. After emptying each box, rinse the inside with clean water.

- **Beware of a February thaw.** If a hard frost follows, plants with shallow roots may be lifted from the ground.

- **Continue looking for plant damage in the garden.** Walk on paths where possible. Press soil around heaved plants, and cut off broken twigs. Where needed, mulch beds with additional evergreen boughs. They can give shallow-rooted plants enough protection to keep them in the ground.

TIP Houses for Birds Birds haven't yet begun their spring rush for real estate, so now is a good time to consider adding birdhouses to your garden. The type of house, entrance-hole size, and placement, have a big effect on the species you are likely to attract. Whether you buy or build birdhouses, look for designs that are fairly easy to clean; old nests should be removed annually. To discourage mice and other creatures from moving into post-mounted houses, make a cone-shaped baffle out of aluminum flashing material, and mount it on the pole below the house, wide-end down. Here are some suggestions for attracting popular species:

- Houses with an entrance hole that measures 1¼ inches will attract a delightful variety of small birds, including house wrens, black-capped chickadees, and nuthatches.

- Bluebirds, tree swallows, and even great-crested flycatchers will move into houses with oval holes that measure 2¼ inches tall and 1⅜ inches wide or round holes that measure 1½ inches (for mountain and western bluebirds, 1⁹⁄₁₆ inches). The size of the hole is important, since starlings, for instance, cannot fit into a house with the above hole sizes. While aggressive house sparrows can easily fit into bluebird houses, they can be discouraged by models that are open at the top and covered with hardware cloth. Bluebirds like the "sun roof." Avoid using a house with a perch on the front; it will encourage house sparrows to take up residence.

- Robins, barn swallows, and phoebes will build on nesting shelves, which have a top and bottom, semi-open sides, and an open front. For kestrels, screech owls, and even flying squirrels, consider putting up a house with a 3-inch round hole.

TREES AND SHRUBS

- **Prune off broken twigs and branches on shrubs.** Keep in mind that pruning spring-flowering shrubs at this time of year will preempt this year's blossoms. Remove broken branches at the point where they join another branch or cut them to the ground. So the blooms don't go to waste, try forcing broken branches removed from spring-blooming shrubs such as forsythia or witch hazel. Always make clean cuts with sharp pruning tools.

- **Prune trees, except for birches, flowering cherries, maples, horse chestnuts, lindens, and walnuts.** The sap of these trees starts to run, or bleed, in late winter and early spring. Wounds that bleed are unattractive; excessive bleeding can weaken the plant and open it to pest or disease problems.

20   *Garden Almanac*

FLOWERING SHRUBS

If only fresh flowers will satisfy your yearning for color, cut some stems off flowering shrubs in late winter, and force them into early bloom indoors. Some flowers, in fact, look better indoors than growing naturally in the landscape. The yellow forsythia that looks so banal in your neighbor's front yard looks brilliant when you force a bunch of stems in a tall cut-glass vase.

When choosing stems for cutting, remember that the earlier a shrub blooms outdoors, the quicker it will come into bloom indoors and vice versa. Thus white forsythia (*Abeliophyllum distichum*), Korean forsythia (*Forsythia ovata*), and border forsythia (*Forsythia × intermedia*) would show fairly quick results, since they bloom in April. By forcing stems, you can bring a wide range of colors to your indoor space. Winter jasmine (*Jasminum nudiflorum*) has bright yellow flowers, and witch hazels (*Hamamelis* spp.) come in a variety of colors ranging from the yellow of native *H. vernalis* to the copper of *H. × intermedia* 'Jelena' and coppery red of 'Diane'. Flowering quince (*Chaenomeles speciosa*), shown at right, is available in cultivars with white, pink, red, or orange flowers, while crab apples (*Malus* spp.) bear flowers in white and shades of pink. Pussy willow (*Salix caprea*), on the other hand, is notable not for flowers but for its silvery gray male catkins that are soft to the touch. Experiment with other spring-flowering shrubs to see which you prefer indoors.

To force branches of these shrubs into bloom, cut long stems, split or crush the bottoms with a hammer, and put them in a container filled with clean tepid water.

Change the water weekly to ensure continued cleanliness. Stems flower faster in a warm room than a cold one, but keep the container away from direct sources of heat. Topping up the container every few days with a little warm water also helps speed the branches into bloom. If you want to delay the flowering of cut stems, add cold water to your container. Keep it in a cold basement or garage until you're ready to bring the stems into bloom.

FLOWERS AND GRASSES

■ **Continue keeping houseplants in topnotch shape by pinching, turning, and cleaning them.** Shape houseplants by pinching back the growth tips and turning them a quarter-turn per week. Keep them clean with a spray bottle or occasional showers.

■ **Water indoor plants sparingly— and avoid fertilizing them altogether—until you see signs of active growth.** Until you see indoor plants pushing out new leaves, water them thoroughly but infrequently with room-temperature water. After you see signs of new growth, such as new leaves or shoots, feed with a weak solution of a balanced fertilizer.

■ **Wrap houseplants carefully if you have to take them outdoors.** When you buy plants from a supermarket or garden center, carry them straight to your warm car and go directly home.

Hyacinth glasses make it easy to force bulbs in water. Buy special prechilled bulbs, or condition your own by storing them in the refrigerator for 3 months before forcing.

■ **Avoid excessive salt use on icy paths.** Use sand or a handful of fertilizer instead.

TIP Propagating Geraniums

You can propagate geraniums for late-spring planting by taking stem cuttings. This technique works with regal geraniums, shown at right, as well as popular zonal or bedding geraniums and pungent-leaved scented types. Cut about 3 inches from the tips of shoots (the equivalent of about 5 leaf nodes). Choose shoots that do not have buds or flowers, if possible, or remove them. Then strip off the lower leaves. Before placing the cuttings into sterile growing medium, dry them overnight (8 to 9 hours). This seals the bases of the cuttings and helps prevent fungal diseases that can rot their roots and stem. Pot up cuttings in clean pots filled almost to the rim with sterile potting medium—a mix of 1 part perlite to 1 part vermiculite works well. Water them in. Avoid overwatering, but mist the cuttings occasionally, and give them cool temperatures (60° to 65°F) and good ventilation.

FRUITS AND VEGETABLES

■ **Plan your vegetable seed-sowing strategy.** Spring can be a busy time in the garden, so before the spring rush begins, sit down with a calendar and all your seed packets and plot out what to sow and when. Some crops are easy— you'll sow them once in spring, either indoors or out. To schedule these, just jot the name of the crop down on your calendar on the best sowing date. With others—such as fast-growing crops like lettuce, mesclun, or spinach—you can extend the harvest by sowing new crops every 3 to 4 weeks. Write the names of these crops on several potential sowing dates. If you like, jot down transplant dates as well. Post your seed-sowing strategy calendar in a prominent place, so you can easily keep on top of which crops need attention.

■ **Begin sowing leek seeds indoors.** Depending on the cultivar, leeks take 100 or more days to mature after they are transplanted outside. For example, 'Laura' is cold tolerant and takes 115 days, 'Otina' takes 120, and 'Titan' 110 days to mature. Starting early is a good idea because the bigger the transplant, the better it will do in the garden.

■ **Prune fall-bearing raspberries in late February.** Cut old fruited canes to the ground. Hardy fall bearers are 'Heritage', 'August Red', and 'Fall Red'. (Prune summer-fruiting cultivars after harvesting.)

Raspberry 'Heritage'.

*Garden*Magic

STARTING SEEDS

If you've never tried starting seeds indoors, now's the time to begin. Few things are more satisfying than the sight of seedlings emerging from the soil to reach for light. Frail or robust, they are a microcosm of life itself—the fittest transplants make it into the garden while the

weak are rousted from the seed tray with a flick of the wrist. Starting seeds indoors gives cold-climate gardeners a jump on the growing season, making it possible to grow flowers and vegetables that wouldn't be productive in areas with short growing seasons. For gardeners in warmer climates, sowing indoors allows annuals to bloom earlier and longer. To start seeds indoors, you need the following:

The phone number of your local Cooperative Extension Service. Your extension agent knows the last frost date for your area. You'll need to know that date to schedule sowing times for all of your seedlings, and to determine when it's safe to transplant seedlings into the garden.

Seed packets. Not only do they hold seeds, but they also contain crucial information, including how and when to sow the seeds and the number of days until germination. Determine from the packet the number of weeks the seeds need from sowing to transplanting. If they need warm, settled weather for transplanting, count back from the last frost date to figure the correct sowing date in your area. Always note the date on the seed packet, since seeds stored in cool, dry conditions may be viable longer than one season.

Containers, including pots, cells, and trays. Purchase pots, cell-packs, or trays from a garden center or use recycled containers from the plastic yogurt, Jello, and pudding cups that find their way into your children's lunch boxes. Be sure plastic containers are clean and have drainage holes; if your recycled containers lack drainage holes, punch them yourself with a nail. Peat pots and homemade newspaper pots are other good options, and can go right into the garden, assuring the integrity of the transplants. You can also buy compressed peat pellets—a combination of pot and soil—that expand when soaked in water. To start seeds, use a container with a depth of about 2 inches to allow for some root development. For easy handling, set containers in flats.

Germinating mix. Using a sterile, soilless, seed-starting medium helps avoid damping off. (Don't use ordinary potting soil for germinating seeds.) Soilless mixtures usually contain some combination of peat moss, sphagnum moss, perlite, and vermiculite. When seedlings have their first set of true leaves, begin fertilizing them with a weak solution of fish emulsion on a regular basis, since seed-starting mixes contain few nutrients.

Light. In northern climates, where winter and early-spring days are short, you may have to provide artificial light for germination. Clean, south-facing windows that don't have light-dimming shades give the best natural light, but be careful that seeds and seedlings don't get too hot. Fluorescent tubes, suspended 2 to 3 inches above seed trays and raised higher as seedlings grow taller, provide adequate light for seedlings in dark rooms or basements. Special grow lights are available, but not necessary. Buy a timer to turn lights on and off.

Water. Seeds and seedlings need an even supply of water to germinate, but seed-starting medium can be difficult to moisten. For best results premoisten it with warm water in a large container, then fill your containers. Gently press down the medium with your fingers and let it drain for a few hours before sowing seeds. Sow the seeds on top, and cover them with the amount of medium recommended on the seed packet. Large seeds often need to be covered for germination, while tiny seeds, and seeds that need light to germinate, are best sown on the surface of the soil. Watering seeds from the top can bury them or wash them away, as well as cause damping off that rots seedlings at the soil line. Instead, water from below by setting containers in a tray filled with room-temperature water, removing them when the moisture soaks to the soil surface. Before watering, check to see if the surface of the medium is dry. Lifting a seed tray also indicates its moisture content—the lighter the

  Garden Almanac

tray, the likelier the soil is dry and ready for watering. Keep the growing medium moist but not wet, and consider making a temporary greenhouse by slipping the tray into a plastic bag until germination occurs. Remove the bag after germination, keeping the seedlings away from the plastic to prevent rot.

Warmth. To increase the rate of germination, place seed trays on an electric heating mat and warm the soil to about 70°F. Once the seeds have germinated, remove them from the mat. Or, place the trays on top of the refrigerator. Be sure not to let the medium dry out; for best results, it needs to remain moist, but not wet.

Patience. Some seeds—like asparagus, angelica, leeks and ornamental onions (*Allium* spp.), coleus, and impatiens—are slow to germinate. Starting seeds of lisianthus (*Eustoma grandiflorum*) is difficult and painstaking but worth the effort for its beautiful red, pink, blue, white, or bicolor flowers, which last a long time when cut. At my house, we've tried lisianthus (also known as prairie gentian) twice with no success, but we've already purchased our seed packets to try again this season. I picture a crock of intense 'Echo Mid Blue' gentians on my kitchen table, and I know I'll seed them each year until my cutting garden is full of them.

MARCH'S TASKS

THE WHOLE GARDEN

- Look out for killing frosts, especially following a thaw, and mulch unprotected plants.
- If you don't know already, find out what the last spring frost date is for your area.
- Begin sowing those seeds that will need 8 to 10 weeks indoors before transplanting.
- Test and tune up gasoline-powered equipment.

TREES AND SHRUBS

- Continue removing snow from shrubs, especially evergreens.
- Continue pruning dormant trees.
- Renewal-prune shrubs flowering on new wood and shrubs grown for colorful stems.
- Don't prune spring-blooming shrubs, except to correct problems.
- Top-dress roses and shrubs with well-rotted manure.
- Transplant young shrubs lacking well-established root systems before the buds swell.
- Control overwintering pests with horticultural oil before the buds swell on trees, shrubs, and vines.

FLOWERS AND GRASSES

- Keep off frozen grass as much as possible.
- Continue inspecting houseplants and plants overwintered indoors for pests and diseases.
- Fertilize early-flowering bulbs as they emerge.

FRUITS AND VEGETABLES

- Continue sowing leek seeds indoors.
- Sow seeds to start pepper transplants.
- Start cabbage, broccoli, and cauliflower transplants.
- Finish pruning fall-bearing raspberries.
- Prune blueberries, currants, and fruit trees.
- At the end of the month, or when the earth is crumbly, till the vegetable garden.

Spring bulbs dominate this month's English bouquet, with daffodils, hyacinths, fritillarias, tulips, and anemones creating a tableau of bright colors. The only way I'll have these bulbs in my New Hampshire bouquet now is to force them or buy them at a florist or supermarket. And why not indulge? A dozen cut daffodils in a crystal vase light up any room. Massed pots of crocuses, daffodils, hyacinths, or tulips look great on wide windowsills and last for a couple of weeks. Enough of dried flowers and grasses! I crave color—fresh blues, cheery yellows, and vibrant reds and greens. Two more months of potentially cold, wet weather make this the time for indulgence, so go ahead: Banish winter's ghost and let spring arrive indoors.

Although hardy bulbs such as daffodils and tulips are planted in fall, there's no better time to begin planning

rch

for them than now. To ensure a long and spectacular display next spring, start a list of what bulbs bloom in your garden this season. Note exactly when each plant blooms, its location in the garden, and what colors are springing up. In late summer and fall, when the bulb catalogues arrive, look for species and cultivars that will add color when and where you need it most. For extra-early flowers, consider snow crocuses (*Crocus chrysanthus*), winter aconites (*Eranthis* spp.), and snowdrops (*Galanthus* spp.) and plant them in a protected spot that warms up early in spring. Careful selection is the secret to extending the bloom time of daffodils and tulips from early spring to almost early summer. Order a selection of cultivars described in catalogues as "early," "midseason," and "late."

1 Royal Widow Auricula.
2 Dwarf white starry Hyacinth.
3 White Bostamon Narciss.
4 High Admiral Anemone.
5 Rhyven Narcys.
6 White passe flower.
7 White grape flower.
8 The lesser black Hellebore.
9 Panax Auricula.
10 White flowering Almond.
11 Dwarf blew starry Hyacinth.
12 American flowering Maple.
13 Goldfinch Polyanthos.
14 Larger blew starry Hyacinth.
15 Virginian flowering Maple.
16 Narciss of Naples.
17 Rose Claremont Tulip.
18 The checker'd Fritillaria.
19 Large leav'd Norway Maple.
20 Double pulchra Hyacinth.
21 Queen of France Narcish.
22 Peltz duré flame Tulip.
23 Blew Oriental Hyacinth.
24 Single bloody Wall.
25 Admiral blew Anemone.
26 Bell Baptico Anemone.
27 Monument Anemone.
28 Red flowering Larch tree.
29 Blew passe flower.
30 Rose Jonker Anemone.
31 White flowering Larch tree.
32 Purple strip'd Anemone.
33 The Velvet Iris.
34 Jerusalem Cowslip.

MARCH

Designed by Pr. Casteels.

From the Collection of Rob't Furber gardener at Kensington 1730.

Engrav'd by H. Fletcher.

Spring comes especially early to my daughter Molly's garden, located on the south side of our house in a corner formed by the angle of the kitchen and the sunroom. Here, protected by walls and warmed by the sun, nubs of sedum sprout from the earth and bulb foliage peeks out of the ground, while the rest of our garden is still barren. March marks the transition between winter and spring: Snow covers the ground during part of the month, but on some days a damp, fresh smell of spring permeates the air, hinting at good things to come. There's still time to prune dormant shrubs and trees and to check for the effects of freezing and thawing, but sowing flower and vegetable seeds becomes more important as the month progresses.

THE WHOLE GARDEN

■ **Look out for killing frosts, especially following a thaw, and mulch unprotected plants.** In wintertime, snow insulates your garden from fluctuating temperatures, but when that blanket melts, in early spring, the plants are left unprotected. A hard freeze after the snow has melted can wreak havoc in the garden, damaging plants that have begun to sprout, killing buds on spring-blooming shrubs—especially those with borderline hardiness like forsythia (*Forsythia* × *intermedia*, Zone 5)—or destroying emerging bulbs of borderline hardiness like ornamental onion (*Allium giganteum*, Zone 6). A hard frost can also lift shallow-rooted perennials and shrubs right out of the soil. Listen closely to weather reports. If severe temperatures are predicted after a prolonged thaw, consider laying evergreen boughs or straw over any exposed and vulnerable plants or garden beds. Pay careful attention to

Snapdragon 'White Bells'.

the winter hardiness of plants you grow, and cultivate only those hardy in your area.

- **If you don't know already, find out what the last spring frost date is for your area.** To determine the optimum time to sow and transplant flowers and vegetables, you'll need to know the last spring frost date. Call your local Cooperative Extension Service office for this information.

- **Begin sowing those seeds that will need 8 to 10 weeks indoors before transplanting.** Snapdragons, coleus, perennial tickseeds (*Coreopsis* spp.), statice (*Limonium* spp.), and verbenas all fall into this category.

- **Test and tune up gasoline-powered equipment.** Make sure lawnmowers, tillers, weed trimmers, leaf blowers, and chainsaws all are in proper working order after several months in storage. If you didn't do preventive maintenance last autumn, now is the time to sharpen the blades, change the oil, and install clean fuel and air filters. Check your safety equipment, too—earmuffs for hearing protection, safety glasses to protect your eyes, and covered shoes for foot safety.

TREES AND SHRUBS

- **Continue removing snow from shrubs, especially evergreens.** A heavy, wet spring snowfall can be especially damaging. Flat-topped evergreen shrubs and hedges are particularly susceptible to snow damage, since snow accumulates quickly on flat surfaces. Brush the snow away before it has a chance to harden and split the plant's fine surface branches.

- **Continue pruning dormant trees.** Remove dead, damaged, or wayward growth, and rubbing or crossing branches. Hire an expert arborist to prune large and valuable specimens. Avoid pruning trees that bleed.

- **Renewal-prune shrubs flowering on new wood and shrubs grown for colorful stems.** Thin out about ⅓ of the oldest wood on shrubs such as beautyberry (*Callicarpa* spp.) and rose-of-Sharon (*Hibiscus syriacus*), as well as shrubs grown for their colorful stems such as red osier dogwood (*Cornus sericea*). Butterfly bush (*Buddleia davidii*) is often killed to the ground in the North, but it blooms on new wood from late summer into fall. Cut plants to the ground in early spring, after the buds have begun to break. Save the slender, sturdy stems for "pea-staking" perennials later in the season.

- **Don't prune spring-blooming shrubs, except to correct problems.** Wait to do major pruning on spring-blooming shrubs until after they have flowered, but cut back long shoots and remove dead wood anytime. Cutting back overly long shoots enhances a shrub's shape and encourages branching. Also remove any branches that rub or cross each other; take out the weaker branch.

- **Top-dress roses and shrubs with well-rotted manure.** Make sure the manure, a ubiquitous organic fertilizer, is old—composted manure, or manure from a heap that has been sitting for at least a year is perfect. Fresh manure, especially when applied in early spring, actually harms plants, as it gives off ammonia. Well-rotted manure, on the other hand, not only contains nitrogen, phosphorus, and potassium, but it also improves the soil structure and adds essential organic matter.

Spring-blooming azaleas, lilacs, and viburnums.

- **Transplant young shrubs lacking well-established root systems before the buds swell.** Dig dormant shrubs bare-root or with a ball of soil. Be sure to have the new hole ready so that you can replant quickly. Transplanting on a cloudy, windless, humid day helps prevent root moisture loss.

- **Control overwintering pests with horticultural oil before the buds swell on trees, shrubs, and vines.** Horticultural oil—also known as superior, supreme, dormant, or summer oil—provides effective, environmentally friendly pest control by smothering pests (such as scale, aphids, mites, and mealybugs) and sparing beneficial insects—if the spraying is properly timed. Be sure to follow label precautions: Horticultural oils can be used in winter at a dormant-season dilution or in summer at a more dilute growing-season rate. Also, the oil should not be sprayed on blue-needled evergreens such as blue spruce (*Picea pungens* f. *glauca*), its cultivars such as 'Hoopsii', or other plants listed on the label, as it dissolves the whitish wax coating that gives their needles a bluish cast. New growth will be blue, but sprayed needles will look even greener in contrast.

FLOWERS AND GRASSES

- **Keep off frozen grass as much as possible.** Frozen blades can break when trampled, and continuous heavy traffic in one area of frozen lawn may eventually cause it to die.

- **Continue inspecting houseplants and plants overwintered indoors for pests and diseases.** Check each time you water for telltale signs like stem-rot and

Snow crocuses (*Crocus chrysanthus*) bloom in late winter to early spring, before the more popular Dutch crocuses.

sticky, yellowing, discolored, or distorted foliage. Inspect and avoid pest-infested plants at the store, and segregate new purchases when you bring them home until you're sure that they are healthy. If you discover a problem with an indoor plant, either treat or discard the plant immediately, depending on the nature of its malaise.

■ **Fertilize early-flowering bulbs as they emerge.** If you didn't top-dress bulbs in fall, feed them now with a balanced fertilizer. Avoid high nitrogen, lawn-type fertilizers which encourage foliage rather than flowers.

TIP Naturalizing Daffodils

Daffodils naturalized in a lawn make a lovely sight in spring. To keep them healthy and blooming from year to year, delay mowing the grass until the daffodil foliage turns yellow. This can be from June until August, depending on where you live, so plantings like this one are best in semi-wild parts of the garden—not where you want a manicured lawn. For the first cutting of the year, you may need to use a string trimmer to cut the grass back to lawnmower height.

■ **Continue sowing leek seeds indoors.** Suitable cold-tolerant varieties range from 'King Richard'—ready to harvest in 75 days—and 'Laura'—an excellent late-harvest leek that matures in 115 days—to 'Giant Musselburgh', a large heirloom leek that produces an edible shank that is 12 inches long and 2 to 3 inches wide.

■ **Sow seeds to start pepper transplants.** To have good-sized transplants for the garden, sow seeds indoors in late March or about 8 weeks before the last frost date. Seedlings of most peppers germinate in about 2 to 3 weeks at temperatures of 80° to 85°F.

'Lyon' leeks.

■ **Start cabbage, broccoli, and cauliflower transplants.** Start these cold-tolerant crops indoors 4 to 6 weeks before they can be planted out in the garden. Hardened-off transplants can be moved to the garden as soon as the soil is workable—3 to 4 weeks before the last frost date.

■ **Prune blueberries, currants, and fruit trees.** Cut away dead, diseased, or pest-infested branches, along with those that rub and cross, while the plants are dormant. Also remove energy-sapping water shoots from their bases. On established shrubs, remove weak or unproductive branches. When pruning to a bud, cut just above it (¼ inch) at a 45-degree angle, and slant the cut down and away from the top of the bud.

■ **At the end of the month, or when the earth is crumbly, till the vegetable garden.** For best results, work compost and/or

rotted manure into the soil whenever you till. Do a soil test. The pH should be between 6 and 7.

Pepper plants (*Capsicum* spp.) are as pretty as they are tasty. They bear white flowers and handsome leaves ranging from grassy to dark green and seductive blackish purple. Best of all, their shiny fruits come in a rainbow of colors. Sweet peppers are especially bright, but many gardeners know them only at the green stage, before they turn technicolor. If you wait 2 or 3 weeks to harvest, you can enjoy their mature hue both in the garden and in the kitchen.

Gardeners in short-season climates need to consider the "days to maturity" when choosing pepper seeds. That's because peppers are heat-lovers and many cultivars take 70 or more days from transplanting until they're ready to harvest green. Even when started indoors and planted out at the earliest suitable date, these late-ripening types barely reach their fully colored maturity before the growing season ends. One of the earliest sweet bell peppers is 'Ace', a productive hybrid that can be harvested green in 50 days; red in 70. 'Gypsy Hybrid', an All-America Selections winner

*Garden*Bounty

PLANT A RAINBOW OF PEPPERS

resistant to tobacco mosaic virus, matures at 65 days. (If you smoke, wash your hands before handling peppers, since you can transmit this virus through touch.) Like 'Ace', 'Sweet Chocolate' peppers tolerate cold weather and make good container plants. They turn green in 58 days; brown in 78. Short-season bell-type peppers available in other colors include 'Islander', which turns lavender in 56 days, and 'Secret', which takes 60 days to turn purple. 'Ivory Charm' ripens creamy white before it turns orange. Another orange pepper, 'Hungarian Sweet Banana', is named for its tapering shape. This sugary, thin-walled cultivar, which is not a bell type, matures to yellow in 52 days and later ripens to orange.

Pepper seeds germinate best in soil kept at 80° to 85°F—much warmer than the 70°F that most popular garden plants require. Starting peppers is a good excuse to buy an electric germination unit, or heat mat, which will raise the soil temperature by 10° to 15°F and boost germination rates. Also use a heat mat for other heat-loving seeds like potatoes, tomatoes, tomatillos, and eggplants—fellow members of the nightshade (*Solanaceae*) family. Without heat, germination is slow and spotty.

Don't start peppers too early, since old leggy transplants make weak garden plants. Short, stocky transplants do best outdoors. Because peppers are heat lovers, they benefit from a sunny location, plenty of water, and black plastic mulch to pre-warm the soil and keep down weeds.

*Garden*Palette

PLANNING A BUTTERFLY GARDEN

What do butterflies want? Adult butterflies have needs similar to our own. The survival of their species depends on attaining the warmth of the sun, food to eat, shelter from the elements, and a safe place to raise their kids. Sunlight is crucial to cold-blooded butterflies—it keeps their wings supple, in turn keeping them airborne. Butterflies also need protection from the wind. Accommodate them by enclosing part of the garden with walls or hedges, or sheltering it with plantings of evergreen or deciduous trees and shrubs.

Butterflies feed on nectar, and thanks to receptors on their feet, tongues, and antennae, they have an acute sense of taste and smell. Yet before these insects become the fluttery, decorative, nectar-sippers that enhance our gardens, they exist as eggs, caterpillars, and chrysalises. Enhanced sensitivity to the needs of these delightful creatures will enable you to transform your garden into a butterfly haven. Butterflies prefer yellow or purple flowers, and a sweet scent adds to the allure. Don't stop at adding nectar plants to beds and borders, though; it's also important to include host or larval food plants, which beckon to egg-laying females and the males that court them. Once the eggs hatch into caterpillars, they eat the host plants on which they were laid. Keep in mind that insecticides designed to kill ravenous caterpillars also destroy the butterflies you want to attract: Green-and-black-striped parsleyworms, which eat parsley, carrots, and dill, hatch into glorious swallowtail butterflies, for example. Dedicate a few plants for caterpillar consumption rather than eradicating them altogether from your property. Butterflies also sometimes drink sap from broken twigs, juice from fruits rotting on the ground, and liquid from dead animals and excrement, so leave a little mess to give your garden extra appeal. Some species also overwinter in leaf litter, so don't rake the garden *completely* clean in fall.

Most gardeners create their butterfly gardens by selecting flowers, but many trees and shrubs also make outstanding butterfly plants and are ideal additions to hedges and other plantings designed to shelter butterflies from the wind. Surprisingly, many common shade trees are important plants for butterflies and their larvae, including aspens and poplars (*Populus* spp.), willows (*Salix* spp.), buckeyes (*Aesculus* spp.), serviceberries

(*Amelanchier* spp.), birches (*Betula* spp.), apples and crab apples (*Malus* spp.), cherries and plums (*Prunus* spp.), and oaks (*Quercus* spp.). Also consider the trees and shrubs listed below for your butterfly garden.

Amur privet (*Ligustrum amurense*) measures 6 to 12 feet high, tolerates pollution, and has creamy white, smelly flowers. It makes an effective clipped hedge.

Blueberries (*Vaccinium* spp.) bear white to pinkish flowers in May that attract butterflies, followed by fruits that attract birds. Highbush blueberry (*V. corymbosum*) grows up to 12 feet high while lowbush blueberries (*V. angustifolia*) can be as short as 5 inches.

Butterfly bush (*Buddleia davidii*) bears trusses of lilaclike flowers that attract flocks of monarchs, swallowtails, and other species. In my garden, both 'Nanho Purple' and 'Pink Delight' are favorites, each measuring about 5 feet tall. To make sure you buy the color you want, purchase one in bloom at the nursery. (I bought a yellow one out of bloom and it turned out to be purple.) Butterfly bush flowers also come in white, blue, magenta red, and dark purple, some with orange eyes.

Eastern redbud (*Cercis canadensis*) is a tree about 30 feet tall with reddish purple buds opening to purplish pink flowers in March or April. It grows in acid or alkaline soils.

Elderberries (*Sambucus* spp.) bear flat trusses of white flowers in midsummer, followed by red to purple-black fruit relished by a variety of songbirds. American elder (*S. canadensis*) reaches 12 feet, while European red elder (*S. racemosa*) reaches 10 feet.

Fragrant sumac (*Rhus aromatica*), smooth sumac (*R. glabra*), and staghorn sumac (*R. typhina*) are suckering, acid-loving shrubs or small trees grown in the wild garden for dramatic fruit and fall color. While cultivars of fragrant sumac are as short as 2 feet, staghorn sumac grows up to 25 feet high in the home landscape.

Japanese pagoda tree (*Sophora japonica*) bears foot-long panicles of fragrant creamy white pea flowers from July through mid-August, and is drought- and pollution-tolerant.

Lilac (*Syringa vulgaris*) and its cultivars reach 15 feet in height and attract moths and butterflies in May to their white, violet, blue, lilac, pink, magenta, purple, or yellow flowers. The downside of lilacs is the powdery mildew that often mars the leaves by midsummer.

Mock orange (*Philadelphus* spp.) bears old-fashioned, sweetly fragrant white flowers in early June on shrubs 10 to 12 feet high.

Native pinxterbloom azalea (*Rhododendron periclymenoides*) has whitish, pink, or deep violet flowers on acid-loving shrubs up to 10 feet tall.

Petite shrubby cinquefoil (*Potentilla fruticosa*) grows up to 4 feet tall, with cultivars bearing yellow, orange, pink, white, red, cream, and salmon blooms from June until frost.

Spring

. . . The garden awakens. Shoots,
turgid with life, emerge from
warming soil. Bluebirds are busy
building nests.

APRIL'S TASKS

THE WHOLE GARDEN

- Begin digging new garden beds when the soil is workable.
- Prepare the soil for seeds.
- Start weeding your beds.
- Water newly planted trees, shrubs, flowers, and vegetables frequently.
- Remove winter mulch when growth begins.

TREES AND SHRUBS

- Remove the compost mounded over the base of your roses as the weather warms.
- Plant bare-root roses when the soil is workable.
- Prune repeat-blooming roses when the buds begin to swell.
- Dig up and replant rooted suckers from own-root shrubs and roses.
- Replant new shrubs and trees that have heaved out of the soil.
- Finish transplanting shrubs before the buds swell.
- Plant shrubs, trees, and vines you purchased balled-and-burlapped or in containers.
- Tidy the mulch in your shrub beds, adding more where necessary.
- Prune shrubs grown for interesting summer leaves or winter stems.

FLOWERS AND GRASSES

- Replant frost-heaved perennials.
- Cut back ornamental grasses and sedum 'Autumn Joy'.
- Transplant and divide summer- and fall-blooming perennials.
- Clean up ground-cover beds and divide overcrowded plants to give them room.
- Add a layer of finished compost to your flowerbeds.
- Sow seeds of hardy annuals and perennials outdoors.
- Plant pansies and other cold-tolerant annuals.
- Harden-off hardy and half-hardy seedlings.
- Repair the lawn by sowing grass seed or laying patches of sod.

FRUITS AND VEGETABLES

- Begin planting asparagus roots in early to mid-spring.
- Lay planting rows with black polyethylene or fiber mulch.
- Direct-seed peas, fava beans, and beets.
- Direct-seed onions and shallots as soon as the soil can be worked.
- Direct-seed lettuce, endive, escarole, and spinach.
- Sow radishes throughout the season, beginning now.
- Move broccoli, cabbage, and cauliflower transplants into the garden.
- Start melons, pumpkins, summer squash, and winter squash indoors.
- Start tomatoes indoors.
- Start kitchen herbs indoors, to be transplanted outside.
- Cut back shrubby herbs.

The April Furber bouquet, in its cheerful disarray, comprises tulips, daffodils, anemones, primroses, hyacinth, and lilies of the valley, plus blooming peach and almond branches. While these bulbs, trees, and flowers may be thriving now in England (mostly Zone 8), as well as farther south in this country, they are certainly not growing outdoors where I live (Zone 5). In cold climates, however, you can advance the bulb display by growing them on a south-facing slope or in a warm, protected microclimate. In spring, however, daffodils, hyacinths, and tulips are easy to buy and peach and almond branches can be forced to flower in early April or allowed to bloom naturally in late April to May, depending on your cold-hardiness zone. Dwarf flowering almond (*Prunus glandulosa*) flowers from late April to early May, the plant's only season of interest. Similarly, common peach (*P. persica*) is lovely in flower but hard to grow and hardy only to Zone 6. The tree goes into leaf after the

ril

flowers have bloomed, but late spring frosts can kill the buds and blossoms.

Now is a good time to plant bare-root roses for future bouquets. Fortunately, roses don't have to be difficult to grow if you select stoic and disease-resistant plants. Hardy, floriferous, and, in my experience, impervious to Japanese beetles and blackspot, the climber 'Blaze' bears scarlet blooms all season long. Two low-maintenance ground-cover roses are also favorites: Pale pink 'Baby Blanket', which grows 3 feet tall and 5 feet wide, and creamy white 'Seafoam', 2 feet high and 6 feet wide. These three roses lack significant fragrance, but 'Carefree Beauty', a 4-foot shrub rose, bears big, bright, medium pink flowers that have a powerfully sweet perfume. Add to this its attractive reddish-orange hips, superior cold hardiness, excellent disease resistance, and you have a superb choice for cold-climate gardens.

This month, gardeners move outdoors. Yes, we're still starting seeds inside the house, but now's the time we work the soil, sow cold-tolerant seeds outside, and divide a few perennials and suckering shrubs. Weeds are growing fast and furious in the flowerbeds. The lawn needs care. Yet the weather still fools us, and a hard spring frost can kill off cherished plants and growing bulbs too tender to survive the final cycle of freeze-and-thaw.

THE WHOLE GARDEN

■ **Begin digging new garden beds when the soil is workable.**
Workable soil is neither too wet nor too dry. Ideally, it is crumbly and sticks together when you squeeze a handful, but breaks apart easily with the pressure of your thumb. If your new bed is in the lawn, you may want to use a tool called a *sod lifter* to preserve the grass for reuse elsewhere. After lifting the sod, dig the bed using a shovel or a tiller, and work in plenty of compost or other organic matter. Most tillers turn over soil to a depth of about 9 inches. In heavy clay soils, there is the possibility of hardpan, a subsoil condition caused by clay being so dense that water cannot penetrate it. Water can sit on this hard tray and drown the roots of susceptible plants. Sometimes hardpan is so deep that you can plant above it successfully. Other times, you must dig through it to break the soil up and increase its aeration and drainage.

- **Prepare the soil for seeds.** If you didn't do it last fall, break up dirt clumps now and dig in well-rotted manure or compost to improve the soil's drainage, moisture retention, and fertility.

- **Start weeding your beds.** The sooner you begin regular weeding, the faster you'll get your weeds under control. Make sure you pull out annual weeds before they set seed, or you'll have many more to pull next year.

- **Water newly planted trees, shrubs, flowers, and vegetables frequently.** Established plants usually have root systems wide enough or deep enough to find water in a dry spell. Young or recently moved plants, however, have neither deep nor well-established root systems. If the roots of new plants dry out, they may go into shock and die.

- **Remove winter mulch when growth begins.** Uncover plants—such as perennials that were protected by evergreen boughs or other coverings—once they begin to show signs of life. Also clear the beds of dead leaves and debris deposited by the wind. Uncover all spring-blooming plants.

TREES AND SHRUBS

- **Remove the compost mounded over the base of your roses as the weather warms.** Move it about 3 inches away from the crown, which is where the roots and stem join.

- **Prune repeat-blooming roses when the buds begin to swell.** Repeat bloomers include hybrid teas, grandifloras, and floribundas; if you grow repeat-blooming shrub roses, this pruning is not mandatory. In mild climates, prune these roses in winter rather than early to mid-spring. With shrub roses, you need only remove dead, damaged, spindly, or very old canes to keep the plant vigorous, and prune as necessary to improve

shape. For large shrubs with many flowers, cut back the shoots by one-third, and for smaller shrubs with bigger flowers, prune the canes by one-half. On all roses, take care of crossing or rubbing canes by removing the weaker one. Prune hybrid tea and grandiflora roses severely, leaving only 3 to 6 stout healthy shoots on the plant. In the North, cut these to 1 foot and in the South to about 2 feet. Always make cuts at a 45-degree angle, ¼ inch above an outward-facing bud. The cut should slope down and away from the bud. On any rose, if you see suckers or shoots growing from the rootstock below the bud union, cut them off as close to where they arose from the root as possible. Suckers are usually quite vigorous and will overtake the grafted plant.

■ **Dig up and replant rooted suckers from own-root shrubs and roses.** Some shrubs have a suckering habit. They spread by shoots that emerge from spreading roots in the ground. Rugosa roses (*Rosa rugosa*), fothergilla (*Fothergilla gardenii* and *F. major*), forsythia (*Forsythia × intermedia*), winterberry (*Ilex verticillata*), oakleaf hydrangea (*Hydrangea quercifolia*), and

highbush blueberry (*Vaccinium corymbosum*) are a few of the plants that you can increase in this easy, inexpensive way. When you dig up a sucker, make a clean cut with a sharp transplanting spade and try to keep the sucker's new roots intact. Replant the shoot as quickly as possible in its new location.

■ **Replant new shrubs and trees that have heaved out of the soil.** Freezing and thawing cycles can actually push plants right out of the soil; replant them quickly before the roots dry out and the plant dies.

■ **Finish transplanting shrubs before the buds swell.** The best time to transplant shrubs is when they're dormant, so they can benefit from the root growth that occurs when buds swell in spring. Calm, gray, humid days are the best time for transplanting, since shrub roots dry out quickly when exposed to sun and wind.

■ **Plant shrubs, trees, and vines you purchased balled-and-burlapped or in containers.** Although fall is an ideal time to add woody plants to your garden, you can also plant these in spring after the ground thaws. Remember, however, that spring-planted shrubs, trees, and vines need regular watering all through the summer to support the top-growth that occurs before the roots become established.

■ **Tidy the mulch in your shrub beds, adding more where necessary.** Mulch should be no more than 3 inches deep, since thicker mulch encourages burrowing rodents. Pull mulch at least 2 to 3 inches away from the trunks of trees and the stems of shrubs. Mulch piled against plant stems and tree trunks fosters rot.

Digging In

PLANTING BARE-ROOT ROSES

Chances are, if you buy roses at big chain stores or through mail-order catalogues, the plants will be bare-root. Bare-root roses are shipped dormant from November to May. If you buy bare-root roses through the mail, open the package immediately and check the roots of the plant to make sure they haven't dried out in transit. Fill a bucket with water and soak the plants overnight or for up to a day before planting. Bare-root roses should be balanced in shape with evenly arranged canes and roots.

Although you can plant bare-root roses in either spring or fall, plan to plant them as soon as the forsythia flowers if you live in a cold climate. Do not plant them when the ground is frozen, because the roots won't grow in frozen soil and can freeze, killing the plant in the process.

The key to growing healthy roses is their location. Choose a sunny, well-drained site where no roses or shrubs have previously grown. A new rose planted in an old rose's soil is susceptible to any problems that plagued the previous inhabitant, causing a disorder called *rose sickness*, which results in unhealthy plants. If you must plant a new rose in an old spot, dig a hole 18 inches to 2 feet deep and wide, placing the soil from the hole in a wheelbarrow as you dig. Discard the old soil and fill the hole with fresh topsoil amended with compost, leaf mold, or well-rotted manure. Manure must be at least a year old so that it doesn't burn the delicate feeder roots your rose will grow. Use a ratio of 1 part organic matter to 2 parts soil. Even if you're planting roses in virgin soil, use this same ratio of soil to organic matter. Roses like slightly acid soil with a pH around 6.5, so consider having the soil in your rose bed tested and adjust it accordingly.

Right before planting, cut off damaged canes and broken or blackened roots with clean, sharp pruners. Then backfill the hole with amended soil, mounding it in the center until it's near ground level. Spread the roots evenly over the mound and continue filling in the hole, patting the soil firmly around the roots. When the hole is almost full, water it well to squeeze out any big air pockets in the soil. Where winters are cold, plant the bud union (the swelling above the roots where the rootstock meets the scion on a grafted plant) 2 inches below the soil's surface. In warm climates, the bud union can be 1 or 2 inches above the soil's surface. If you're planting roses grown on their own roots, follow a similar procedure but set the crown, where the roots meet the canes, about 1 inch below ground level. Fill the hole to the top and water it again. Water your roses deeply all summer and into fall, giving them 1 to 2 inches of water per week.

FLOWERS AND GRASSES

- **Replant frost-heaved perennials.** Repeated cycles of freezing and thawing can still heave plants right out of the ground. Replant before they dry out and roots are damaged.

- **Cut back ornamental grasses and sedum 'Autumn Joy'.** Before the new season's growth kicks in, cut back plants kept for winter interest to within several inches of the ground.

- **Transplant and divide summer- and fall-blooming perennials.** Do this when they are about 3 inches high. When replanting, amend the soil with 2 tablespoons of bone meal or wood ashes around each one to improve flowering. If asters have grown woody with age, dig and divide them by cutting young productive shoots and roots off the sides of the clump for replanting. Toss the center of the clump on your compost pile.

- **Clean up ground-cover beds and divide overcrowded plants to give them room.** Cut out dead stems and other winter damage, and remove dead leaves from plants such as lungwort (*Pulmonaria* spp.) and bergenia (*Bergenia cordifolia*). If you wait much longer, pruning may harm the new growth. When *Veronica incana* emerges from the winter doldrums, it can look dull, woody, and frost damaged. After cutting this ground cover back to vital stems and clearing away the resulting debris, dig up rooted sections for dividing. As long as the material is healthy, even the tiniest division of veronica is viable and by fall will be a sturdy plant.

- **Add a layer of finished compost to your flowerbeds.** A 2-inch top-dressing provides nutrients, improves drainage and moisture retention, and helps keep plant roots cool in hot weather. If you grow only annuals in these beds, you may choose to dig the compost into the soil surface.

- **Sow seeds of hardy annuals and perennials outdoors.** Sow foxgloves (*Digitalis purpurea*), bellflowers (*Campanula* spp.), and hollyhocks (*Alcea rosea*). If you didn't sow seeds of annual poppies (*Papaver* spp.) and forget-me-nots (*Myosotis sylvatica*) last fall, sow them now, when the soil begins to warm.

- **Plant pansies and other cold-tolerant annuals.** Pansies, Johnny-jump-ups, snapdragons,

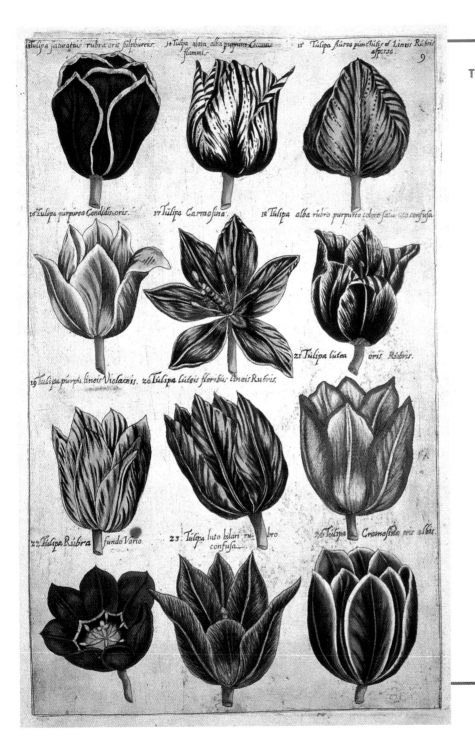

Tulipa januariis rubra oris sulphureis. 14 Tulipa alata alba purpurea Coccineis flammis. 15 Tulipa aurea punctulis et Lineis Rubris aspersa.

9

16 Tulipa purpurea Candidis oris. 17 Tulipa Carmosina. 18 Tulipa alba rubro purpureo colore saturato confusa.

19 Tulipa purpi lineis Violaceis. 20 Tulipa luteis floribus lineis Rubris. 21 Tulipa lutea oris Rubris.

22 Tulipa Rubra fundo Vario. 23 Tulipa luto hilari rubro confusa. 24 Tulipa Cremosula oris albis.

TIP Bulb Care 101 It's easy to feel confused about what to do with bulbs after they've finished blooming. To encourage large hybrid bulbs such as daffodils and tulips to direct energy into next year's flowers, remove the blooms as they fade. (Cut—don't pull—them off, as it's easy to disturb the roots.) Since smaller bulbs often self-sow, leave their flowers if you want seeds to form so you can enjoy the seedlings in years to come. Don't for a minute consider removing the ripening leaves, though, which remain green for several weeks, then turn yellow; they're busy making food for next year's flowers. Wait until the leaves turn completely yellow before removing them. Don't braid or otherwise bundle them either, as this reduces the plant's ability to manufacture food; try interplanting bulbs with perennials such as hostas, so that emerging hosta leaves can help to hide the maturing bulb foliage. Interspersing annuals among ripening bulbs is also effective.

and dusty miller (*Senecio cineraria*) withstand some frost and look good in spring and early fall when the weather is cool. With colors ranging from bright yellow, purple, and blue to white, red, and salmon-pink, pansies in particular bring early color to drab garden beds and cheer up containers by the front door.

■ **Harden off hardy and half-hardy seedlings.** Before moving seedlings of hardy or half-hardy plants to the garden, acclimate them to the harsher conditions outdoors. Set them out in a protected spot for an hour the first day, then gradually increase the amount of time they spend outdoors until they can be left out overnight. Ideally, transplant on a dull, overcast day. Seedlings of hardy perennials and biennials, along with half-hardy, or cool-weather annuals, are good candidates for hardening off this time of year.

■ **Repair the lawn by sowing grass seed or laying patches of sod.** Cover seed repairs with burlap or straw to keep the ground warm and protect the seeds from birds.

FRUITS AND VEGETABLES

■ **Begin planting asparagus roots in early to mid-spring.** Growing asparagus requires preparation but is well worth the effort because an established bed will produce fresh, sweet asparagus for 20 or more years. Asparagus requires deep, well-drained, preferably sandy, weed-free soil enriched with compost or well-rotted manure. Not an acid lover, it likes a pH of

6.5 to 7.5, which you can achieve with an application of limestone or wood ashes during planting. Most catalogues offer 1-year-old roots, and you'll need about 25 of them to provide meal-size portions for harvesting. One year after planting you can harvest a few spears, but from the third year on your harvest should be substantial. 'Jersey Knight' and 'Jersey King' are productive, disease-resistant cultivars.

■ **Lay planting rows with black polyethylene or fiber mulch.** In cold-climate areas, these mulches warm the soil, retain moisture, and suppress weeds, resulting in earlier and more productive harvests. Garden staples may hold the strips down in protected areas, but if you garden on a windy site as I do, weigh the sides down with rocks and bury the edges in soil so they don't fly away at the first gust.

■ **Direct-seed peas, fava beans, and beets.** Sow as soon as the soil can be worked, but avoid soggy soil, which can lead to pea-root rot, a fungus that browns and dries the leaves. Peas are also susceptible to powdery mildew, wilt, and mosaic viruses. To avoid these problems

organically, don't plant peas in the same place more than once every 3 years and plant disease-resistant cultivars in well-drained soil. Try 'Knight', a very early shelling type, and 'Oregon Sugar Pod II' snow pea for disease resistance. Potash, phosphorus, and a pH over 6.0 are important for good yields.

■ **Direct-seed onions and shallots as soon as the soil can be worked.** Be sure to save them a sunny, fertile, well-drained spot rich in organic matter.

■ **Direct-seed lettuce, endive, escarole, and spinach.** Begin now and continue sowing new crops every 2 weeks throughout the summer and fall. Plant heat-tolerant, slow-bolting cultivars for summer harvest, including 'Green Ice', 'Simpson Elite', and 'Red Oakleaf'—all looseleaf lettuces, 'Sierra Blush'—a summer batavia lettuce, 'Deer Tongue' and 'Buttercrunch' bibb lettuce, 'Coral' escarole, 'Tres Fine' curly endive, and 'Hector' spinach.

■ **Sow radishes throughout the season, beginning now.** Sow new crops every 2 to 3 weeks. Pay attention to the cultivars you plant, since white daikon radishes usually bolt when planted in the spring. Radishes need frequent watering for a successful harvest.

■ **Move broccoli, cabbage, and cauliflower transplants into the garden.** All these members of the cabbage family are heavy feeders needing humusy fertile soil, ample water, and a pH higher than 6.0.

TOMATO
JOHN BAER
POMEDORO GROSSO

CARD SEED.CO.
·‹ FREDONIA, N.Y. ›·

■ **Start melons, pumpkins, summer squash, and winter squash indoors.** Small plants transplant best, so wait to sow until 1 to 2 weeks before the last frost date. Transplants should not be more than 4 weeks old.

■ **Start tomatoes indoors.** Sow seeds 6 to 8 weeks before the last frost date. If in doubt, wait to sow, since compact healthy transplants make better plants than spindly, stretched ones.

■ **Start kitchen herbs indoors, to be transplanted outside.** Start basil, garlic chives, chives, cilantro, dill, fennel, lemon grass, and sweet marjoram from seeds. Start with plants or cuttings of oregano, rosemary, sage, summer and winter savory, and thyme.

■ **Cut back shrubby herbs.** Perennial sage, lavender, Greek oregano, French thyme, and French tarragon benefit from a spring trim to stimulate growth.

Garden Almanac

TOMATOES SEE RED

Want to grow more tomatoes than ever before? We all know that mulching them with black plastic warms their roots, saves water, keeps weeds down, and helps the fruit stay clean. *Red* plastic mulch does all that and more. Separate trials by the United States Department of Agriculture, Penn State, and the University of New Hampshire show that when tomatoes are grown with 1 millimeter of a red plastic mulch developed by the USDA, yields increase from 12 to 24 percent and more over crops produced with black plastic. Red plastic also lowers the number of nematodes in the soil because, as it causes the plant to devote more energy to growing *above* ground, less food energy goes to the roots on which nematodes feed.

It sounds like magic, but it's pure science. Red plastic reflects the far-red spectrum of light. These wavelengths make each plant think that similar plants are nearby, thereby fooling them into competing with those other plants for sunlight, nutrients, and space by outgrowing them. Far-red light also triggers a natural growth regulator in the tomato plant, which senses environmental changes in the color of light and sends new growth to the maturing fruit. The plant then puts more energy into its shoots than into its roots, which are coddled by the red plastic mulch. Sadly, red plastic mulch is not widely available. Two sources are the Gardener's Supply catalogue (1-800-863-1700, ask for "tomato booster mulch") and on the Web at An Obscure Gardener, www.obscuregardener.com.

MAY'S TASKS

THE WHOLE GARDEN

- Weed your beds thoroughly before they get out of hand.
- Make sure all winter mulches are removed by the beginning of the month.
- Top off summer mulch in beds where levels have dropped below 2 inches.
- Rake beds that have ample mulch, to prevent matting.
- Keep watering transplants and new plants frequently.

TREES AND SHRUBS

- Prune shrubs that flower in early spring right after they bloom.
- Prune conifers.
- Train topiaries and espaliers.
- Plant potted roses.
- Fertilize roses, if you didn't feed them earlier in the season.

FLOWERS AND GRASSES

- Cut back perennial stems damaged by frost.
- Set out dahlias after the last frost date.
- Plant gladiolus corms beginning early this month.
- Finish dividing summer- and fall-blooming perennials.
- Stake peonies, delphiniums, and tall phlox early.
- Start planting tender annuals outdoors after the last frost date.
- Reseed bare spots in the lawn.

FRUITS AND VEGETABLES

- Start cucumbers indoors.
- Finish planting asparagus roots early in the month.
- Continue sowing onions, carrots, and beets directly in the garden.
- Begin direct-seeding bush and pole beans and corn after the last frost date.
- Direct-seed parsley, which takes 3 weeks to germinate.
- Continue sowing radishes, endive, escarole, lettuce, and spinach every 2 weeks.
- Direct seed chervil, Swiss chard, turnips, and fennel.
- Begin transplanting tomatoes into the garden.
- Begin transplanting pumpkins, melons, and summer and winter squash seedlings into the garden.
- Begin transplanting peppers and eggplants into the garden.
- Start fall crops of broccoli, Brussels sprouts, cauliflower, and cabbage by direct-seeding or starting flats for transplanting in June and July.
- Set herb transplants into the garden.
- Plant strawberries.

May

While late-spring flowers spill over the edges of this month's Furber arrangement, my garden bouquet looks different indeed. This is lilac season, and blooms more glorious in scent and appearance are hard to find. I grow common lilac (*Syringa vulgaris*) at the back of a shrub border, since powdery mildew covers its leaves by summer's end. Its old-fashioned, sweetly-scented lavender flowers perfume my house mid-month, while late-blooming lavender *S. patula* 'Miss Kim' and pink *S.* × *prestoniae* 'James MacFarlane', both foundation plants, scent my front path and make bouquets into June. While the pheasant's eye—among the last of the daffodil bulbs to bloom each year—is blooming in England, in New Hampshire many daffodils are just hitting their stride, bringing sunny yellow, orange, white, and red flowers to Northern gardens and homes. Tulips and true blue scillas (*Scilla* spp.) abound. Lily leeks (*Allium moly*)

and other ornamental onions add more yellow and purple hues to the late-spring bouquet.

In my garden, I make a visual bouquet by planting my 'Miss Kim' and 'James MacFarlane' lilacs behind a low hedge of 'Crimson Pygmy' barberry. The red-purple leaves of the barberry look smashing with the true-pink flowers of 'James MacFarlane'. Moreover, in autumn the foliage of 'Miss Kim' turns dark purplish-red, thus harmonizing splendidly with 'Crimson Pygmy' barberry's deep red fall color. A bluish evergreen backdrop enhances pink- and blue-flowered lilacs. Compact alpine fir (*Abies lasiocarpa* 'Compacta'), Hoops blue spruce (*Picea pungens* 'Hoopsii'), and silver Japanese pine (*Pinus parviflora* 'Glauca') are 3 blue-leaved conifers. Plant lilacs to the south or east of conifers to ensure these flowering shrubs receive plenty of sunlight.

1. Cinamon Rose.
2. Narrow-Leav'd Strip'd flower de-luce.
3. Columbine Strip'd.
4. Bishop of Canterbury Tulip.
5. Double Dutch fly.
6. Late white Hyacinth.
7. Blew-bell Hyacinth.
8. Mountain bulbal Crow foot.
9. Beluluia Anemone.
10. Venetian Vetch.
11. Blew Hyacinth of peru.
12. China pink.
13. Savoy Spider wort.
14. Double Orange Lilly.
15. White Hyacinth of peru.
16. Pheasants Eye.
17. Purple Mallow.
18. Arbor Judæ.
19. Embroidered Cranes bill.
20. Dwarf Dutch Tulip.
21. Indian Queen Ranunculus.
22. Yellow Austrian rose.
23. Double white Mountain Ranunculus.
24. Dutch yellow Ranunculus.
25. Indian King Ranunculus.
26. Yellow globe flower.
27. Red Austrian rose.
28. Cytisus Secundus Clusy.
29. Lotus with yellow flower.
30. Virginian Columbine.
31. White Asphodil.
32. Yellow Asphodil.
33. Princess's Pink.

MAY

From the Collection of Rob.t Furber Gardner at Kensington. 1730.

Dessin'd by P.t Casteels. Engrav'd by H.r Fletcher.

As a schoolgirl in St. Louis, I danced around a maypole to "Spring" from Vivaldi's *Four Seasons* and saw the May Queen crowned. Since maypoles in New Hampshire are often surrounded by knee-deep mud, I've developed a simpler ritual to welcome spring into my life. Early each morning I stroll through my garden, stopping here and there to pull a weed or admire new shoots on perennials. I marvel at the persistence of these plants and of the trees, which leaf out a bit more each day. I mourn the death of a few leafy garden friends and see what needs to be done to keep the rest of my plants healthy and thriving through the growing season.

THE WHOLE GARDEN

■ **Weed your beds thoroughly before they get out of hand.** Summer's annual weeds are still sprouting, and a thorough weeding early in the season will go a long way toward controlling problems later on. If you pull weeds up by hand when the soil is moist, they'll come up easily, roots and all.

■ **Make sure all winter mulches are removed by the beginning of the month.** Winter mulches are managed differently from those designed to control weeds or hold water in the soil. Mulch covers plants to protect them from winter cold and thaw, but once plants start growing in spring, they need light, good air circulation, and growing space to stay healthy. Leaving plants covered with winter mulch also invites damage by slugs and rodents.

■ **Top off summer mulch in beds where levels have dropped below 2 inches.** Organic mulches like shredded bark, compost, straw, or salt-marsh hay eventually decompose and add beneficial organic matter to the soil. To enjoy the continued benefits of mulching—it controls weeds and holds moisture in the soil—add more periodically to keep the layer

Damage Control

DAMAGE CONTROL: DEER

Shouts from my 4-year-old daughter brought me running downstairs. She was standing by the French doors that open onto the patio, watching three deer munch potted flowers only a few feet away. She had already been treated once for Lyme disease, so I knew what peripheral damage these graceful pests can cause. Lyme disease, carried by ticks between deer and field mice, is transferred fairly easily to humans who wander into areas occupied by these common residents of rural and suburban zones.

Short of moving to a plant-free lot, the best way to eradicate deer from your garden is by fencing them out. If it's a particular shrub or tree they like to eat, enclose the tasty plant in chicken wire. A 4-foot-high cage should protect a plant to grazing height. If deer find your whole garden delectable, install a fence that is 8 feet tall to keep them away. If you install a shorter fence, say 3 feet tall, inside the higher fence, you'll confuse them and make their visits even more difficult. Deer are also unlikely to jump a tall, solid barrier, such as a board fence. You can install a strand of electric fencing 2 feet off the ground and 3 feet outside an existing fence. Attach strips of aluminum foil smeared with peanut butter to the electric fencing before activating it. The deer will try to sample the peanut butter and get the "keep away" message loud and clear.

Repellents may also work for a short time. A popular home remedy is to hang bars of strong-smelling soap on plants you want to protect or to suspend the bars every 15 feet around your yard. You can also stud your bushes and trees with mesh bags filled with human hair, or cloth soaked in hot sauce. Hardware stores sell urine-based repellents to squirt on rags near special plants or around the perimeter of your property. If deer are hungry enough, however, they will put up with just about anything for a meal.

Planting deer-resistant plants is often ineffectual, since for every deer-resistant plant, there's a deer somewhere who loves to eat it. Still, you may want to try yarrows (*Achillea* spp.), ornamental onions (*Allium* spp.), anemones (*Anemone* spp.), bergenias (*Bergenia* spp.), barrenworts (*Epimedium* spp.), some hardy geraniums (*Geranium* spp.), hellebores (*Helleborus* spp.), English lavender (*Lavandula angustifolia*), peonies (*Paeonia* spp.), and meadow rues (*Thalictrum* spp.).

Our dogs turn out to be the most effective deterrent against deer. As long as the dogs—a barky corgi and an aggressive Bedlington terrier—are outdoors, they keep the deer at bay.

2 to 3 inches deep. Be sure to keep mulch a few inches away from plant stems, tree trunks, and crowns of perennials, as it can encourage disease and rot.

■ **Rake beds that have ample mulch, to prevent matting.** If you just mulched your beds in the fall, all they need now to keep them looking fresh is a gentle surface raking to break up any crust that may have formed over the winter.

■ **Keep watering transplants and new plants frequently.** Transplants and new plants lack well-established root systems to seek and carry water for their survival. In spring, when plants are experiencing both root and top growth, adequate water is vital to their continued health.

TREES AND SHRUBS

■ **Prune shrubs that flower in early spring right after they bloom.** Spring-flowering shrubs bloom on old wood, meaning they set their flower buds on growth of the previous summer. It's best to prune them right after they flower, because pruning during winter removes flower buds, although it won't hurt the plants. Shrubs and trees to prune this time of year include *Deutzia* spp., *Forsythia* spp., lilacs (*Syringa* spp.), flowering quinces (*Chaenomeles* spp.), pearlbush (*Exochorda* spp.), witch hazels (*Hamamelis* spp.), *Kerria* spp., beautybush (*Kolkwitzia* spp.), spring-blooming magnolias (including *Magnolia stellata* and *M. × soulangiana*), mock oranges (*Philadelphus* spp.), cherries (*Prunus* spp.), *Wiegela* spp., mountain laurels (*Kalmia* spp.), and azaleas and rhododendrons (*Rhododendron* spp.). Remove damaged and diseased growth, rubbing and crossing branches, and clip back wayward growth just above a branch or bud to encourage bushy growth.

■ **Prune conifers.** Conifers such as needled evergreens—like pines and spruces—generally require little to no pruning, except for removing the occasional stray, sick, or dead branch. Actually, you can prune most conifers throughout the year if you're taking branches off close to the trunk. With needled evergreens, branches cut back into needleless older wood generally will not resprout. When possible, avoid pruning the leader or central stem at the top of the plant, since cutting it off will change the tree's

Saucer magnolia
(*Magnolia* × *soulangeana*).

natural habit. Some gardeners, however, trim back the leader by half to force the tree to grow bushy at the sides. If you want to control the size and fullness of pines, spruces, and firs you can prune them in spring after they develop growing tips, called candles, at the end of each branch. Be sure to do this before the needles on the candles harden and spread. Starting in late May in Zone 6 or in June farther north, break ½ to ⅔ of each candle off with your hands. Hand pruning is preferable to shears, which can damage new needles.

■ **Plant potted roses.** This is a good time to buy and plant potted roses. Like bare-root roses, they do best with at least 6 hours of sunlight early in the day and with a well-drained, slightly acid soil. Some roses, however, can put up with less than ideal conditions, for instance heavier and slightly alkaline soil. The more stress on the rose, however, the more likely it is to suffer complications from pests and diseases. Follow directions for bare-root roses but be careful to keep the potting soil around the roots intact when placing the plant in the hole. If necessary, cut the container away

from the plant to keep from disturbing the roots. Water weekly throughout the summer.

■ **Fertilize roses, if you didn't feed them earlier in the season.** Established roses benefit from a 4-inch dressing of aged, well-rotted manure or compost scratched into the soil around the base of the plant anytime from late winter until after growth begins in early spring. Roses are heavy feeders, and this humusy mulch nourishes the soil and helps it stay moist in the growing season. For roses that bloom once a year, this annual feeding should be enough to keep them healthy and beautiful. Top-dress repeat-blooming (remontant) roses like hybrid teas, grandifloras, and some shrub roses in spring, and give them 3 additional feedings during the growing season. Feed after growth begins in the spring, after the first flush of bloom in June, and a third time 6 weeks later. To fertilize, it's easiest to buy a commercial rose food and use it according to the manufacturer's instructions. Rose foods are available in chemical and organic formulas. Once a week, water your roses deeply, preferably with a soaker hose, to keep them flourishing.

*Garden*History

TOPIARY

Topiary, one of the traditional horticultural arts, involves sculpting an object from a living plant. Typically, a topiary has a geometric shape—a cone, an obelisk, a pyramid, or a series of spheres—but gardeners have also pruned plants to resemble chicks, ducks, bears, and trains. One series of topiaries at Ladew Topiary Gardens in Maryland depicts a foxhunt, complete with fox and pack of hounds followed by a horse and rider.

Topiary works best in formal gardens. Set against a background of lawn and sheared hedges, figurative topiaries make whimsical accents or focal points.

Geometric topiaries, on the other hand, have more uses. Not only do they make outstanding points of interest, they also add visual weight to the entrance of a house, a path, or a garden. The topiaries on these pages are from the horticultural beautification program for the Clark Foundation in Cooperstown, New York.

Visible in ancient Egyptian wall paintings, topiary was carried to Italy by the Romans. (The word topiary derives from *topiarius*, the Latin word for a gardener in charge of shrubbery.) After enjoying a vogue in the ancient world, the use of topiary declined in the Middle

Ages. During the Renaissance, however, it was revived in the gardens of affluent homeowners in France, Italy, and Holland. The patron's desire to show absolute dominance over his surroundings went hand-in-hand with the grandiosity of the 17th-century baroque era. Gardens like Louis XIV's at Versailles were designed as symmetrical, walled, formal spaces. In these settings, topiaries often appeared in corners or in the center of garden rooms, lined the sides of water features, or accented scrolled parterres and geometric knot gardens.

English aristocrats in the Tudor and Stuart periods relished their formal gardens studded with topiaries, but the technique eventually fell out of favor. The 18th-century poets Joseph Addison and Alexander Pope publicly disdained what they saw as a perversion of nature. Such criticism encouraged a more naturalistic style of landscaping to replace the custom. This anti-topiary quote from Joseph Addison (1672–1719) in *The Spectator*, in June 1712, reveals their disgust: "We see Marks of the Scissars upon every Plant and Bush. I do not know whether I am singular in my Opinion, but, for my own part, I would rather look upon a Tree in all its Luxuriancy and Diffusion of Boughs and Branches, than when it is thus cut and trimmed into a Mathematical Figure."

By the Victorian period, formal gardens and topiary made a comeback on the grand estates of the nouveau riche, but World War I carried off many of the gardeners who had kept these living sculptures trimmed. Some formal gardens survived, but many more grew unkempt with the passage of time. In villages, however, some cottagers kept the art of topiary alive, creating quaint animals and maintaining ancient hedges.

Through the centuries, English yew (*Taxus* spp.) and boxwood (*Buxus* spp.) have proved to be among the best plants for topiaries because they have small leaves that grow densely when sheared. Moreover, they sprout on old wood, so they can be cut near the ground and will produce fresh new shoots from the base. A woody vine like English ivy (*Hedera helix*), on the other hand, is easy to train over manufactured topiary forms. While English yew and most boxwoods aren't suitable plants for the North (English yew is hardy only to Zone 7 and most boxwoods to Zone 6), there are other choices for cold-climate gardeners. Japanese yew (*Taxus cuspidata*) and some koreana-form cultivars of littleleaf boxwood (*Buxus microphylla* var. *koreana*) are hardy to Zone 4. Spring and fall are good times to plant shrubs for topiaries; the best time to trim them, however, is July.

FLOWERS AND GRASSES

■ **Cut back perennial stems damaged by frost.** This is your last chance to clean up the flower garden before the onset of rapid growth. If late frosts kill tender stems on newly sprouted perennials, clip off the damaged parts at the base, since they can act as a gangway for pests and diseases.

■ **Set out dahlias after the last frost date.** If you want colorful flowers in late summer and fall, plant dahlias in your border after the danger of frost has passed and the soil has begun to warm up. Dahlias are tender, tuberous-rooted plants that vary from compact, foot-tall edgers to behemoths more than 8 feet tall. Blooms range from less than 2 inches to more than 18 inches wide. For the best flowers, give the plants moist, fertile soil in full sun. If you are growing taller types, install sturdy stakes at planting time. Mulching helps retain moisture and warms the soil. If you grow dahlias every year, rotate their location in the garden to keep them disease free.

■ **Plant gladiolus corms beginning early this month.** To ensure a steady supply of flowers for cutting from summer to fall, plant these tender corms every 2 weeks. Glads like rich, well-drained, moist soil and a sunny location, although they tolerate some shade. If their Victorian looks don't harmonize with your garden's style, grow them in a row in the cutting garden. Plant the corms close together (3 to 6 inches apart) and cover them with 2 or 3 inches of soil. Because glads are top-heavy when in bloom, support plants in a cutting garden by pounding in heavy stakes at each corner of your row. Wrap string around one stake, stretch it to the next, and repeat the process until you've made a string-box to hold the plants in place. Glads also benefit from an application of a balanced fertilizer when the flower stalk appears.

■ **Finish dividing summer- and fall-blooming perennials.** To minimize stress on the plants, make sure you do this before they put on significant growth.

■ **Stake peonies, delphiniums, and tall phlox early.** Install cages or other supports when these and other tall perennials are only a few inches high, so plants can grow up

ANNUALS.

through them and hide supports with foliage. If you wait until plants become tall and top-heavy, you may harm the stems by forcing them into a circular frame or damage the roots by hammering a pole stake through them.

■ **Start planting tender annuals outdoors after the last frost date.** In my part of Zone 5, that's between May 20 and 25, but to be absolutely sure it's safe to set out tender plants, we often wait until Memorial Day weekend. For very cold-sensitive annuals, it's often best to wait to transplant until a week or 2 after the last frost date, when the weather has settled and the soil warmed up.

■ **Reseed bare spots in the lawn.** Remove the dead grass and loosen soil with a hard rake, breaking up the top inch. Seed the area with a high-quality grass seed appropriate for your region. Sprinkle a starter fertilizer over the reseeded patch. On small spots, lay burlap down; cover larger areas with weed-free straw. Water deeply, and keep the site moist until the grass is well established. Wait to cut new grass for the first time until it is 2 to 3 inches tall. Cutting boosts root growth.

M a y

Digging In

A garden can be fanciful and work-intensive—a topiary garden filled with jungle and barnyard "animals"—or as simple as a mini-Stonehenge created from granite boulders on a bare side lawn. An essential step toward success is deciding on the amount and type of work your garden should require. Do you think you'd enjoy a planting that requires regular attention? Many gardeners find manicuring a high-maintenance planting such as a topiary or knot garden relaxing and restful; others resent the constant demand of time and attention such plantings require to look their best. When in doubt, start with a garden that is easy to install and requires little care—you can always try something more ambitious next year. Thumb through books and magazines to find plants you like, read plant dictionaries to discover how successfully they might grow in your area, and think about how you'd use them in a garden of your own. Start a scrapbook with your own notes plus pictures and articles from newspapers and magazines. For fun, sketch your ideas in color on a big blank piece of paper.

Build your confidence by growing a few flowers from seed. Nasturtiums and sunflowers, for example, are sun-

loving annuals that grow fast and have brightly colored flowers and edible parts. Sunflowers attract hungry birds and playful squirrels, and nasturtiums bring hummingbirds, which never cease to enthrall. To start a sunflower or nasturtium indoors, simply drop a seed in a Styrofoam cup filled with moistened soil. (For smaller seeds, you can use half a Styrofoam egg carton, popping one seed in each little cup.) Cover the seed with a sprinkling of soil. The cup should have a small drainage hole poked into the bottom. Set the cup on a saucer in a sunlit window and watch the new plant germinate and grow. Start the seeds about 2 weeks before the last frost date and wait until the weather is warm and settled before planting them outdoors. Although this process is easy, the resulting flowers are as varied and sophisticated as store-bought plants. Once the blooms have faded, let a few of the plants set seed. Collect this when it is ripe, for sowing the following year. Place dried seeds in envelopes clearly marked with the name of the plant and date you collected the seed. Store the envelopes in a dark, dry cupboard.

To start an easy garden outdoors, clear a small plot of land and till it, digging in finished compost or well-rotted manure so your plants can flourish. Some people pour bags of soil on top the area they want to garden, then plant seeds or seedlings directly in the fresh soil surface. For even better results, and to encourage plants to put down deeper roots, loosen the soil on the site before pouring new topsoil on top. Consider framing the new garden with boards or bricks to make a raised bed and hold the soil in place.

Sow the site with flower seeds according to the directions on the back of the packet—sunflowers, zinnias, nasturtiums, pot marigolds (*Calendula* spp.), bachelor's buttons (*Centaurea cyanus*), and cosmos (*Cosmos* spp.) are all annuals that can be direct-sown right in the garden. For best effect, sow seeds in drifts of all one plant—as a guide you can draw shapes on the soil with a stick before you sow . You may also want to pop in some small annual starts from a local garden center for instant color. Keep the soil evenly moist with a watering can or a fine spray of water from the hose until seedlings are up and growing. You'll probably need to thin the seedlings and weed regularly, too. Once plants are several inches tall, add a layer of mulch—keep it an inch or so away from plant stems—to control weeds and keep the soil moist.

Consider mixing in some edibles, too. Pumpkins are great if you have lots of space—they even make a nice temporary ground cover under shrubs, as long as you don't let them engulf their bedfellows. Even though pumpkins take a long time to mature (about 85 to 115 days, depending on the cultivar), you can watch their size increase almost daily. Fast-growing radishes provide a different kind of quick gratification: 'D'Avignon', an heirloom radish, is ready to harvest in only 21 days and 'Cherry Belle', an All-America winner, can be harvested in 22. Or consider a mix of leaf lettuces to add frilly, red-and-green color to your instant garden.

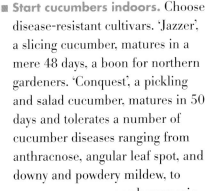

FRUITS AND VEGETABLES

■ **Start cucumbers indoors.** Choose disease-resistant cultivars. 'Jazzer', a slicing cucumber, matures in a mere 48 days, a boon for northern gardeners. 'Conquest', a pickling and salad cucumber, matures in 50 days and tolerates a number of cucumber diseases ranging from anthracnose, angular leaf spot, and downy and powdery mildew, to cucumber mosaic virus and scab. 'Sweet Success', a burpless variety, is an All-America winner maturing in 58 days and is resistant to cucumber and watermelon viruses, scab, and leaf spot. For the highest germination rate, give the seed flats bottom heat to warm the soil to 86°F.

■ **Begin direct-seeding bush and pole beans and corn after the last frost date.** Both bean and corn seeds rot in cold, wet soil. Wait to sow corn until after the soil is warm—at least 65°F. Beans are best sown after the soil reaches 55°F.

■ **Direct-seed parsley, which takes 3 weeks to germinate.** Soaking seeds for 24 hours before planting speeds germination.

■ **Direct-seed chervil, Swiss chard, turnips, and fennel.** Chervil and fennel do not transplant easily, and are best sown where they are to grow. For an early start, Swiss chard can be sown indoors a few weeks before the last frost date. Turnips and turnip greens are best-tasting when grown quickly—with adequate water and rich soil—in cool weather.

■ **Begin transplanting tomatoes into the garden.** Don't move them until night temperatures consistently stay above 50°F. Installing black—or, preferably, red—plastic mulch a week or more before transplanting helps warm the soil.

■ **Begin transplanting pumpkins, melons, and summer and winter squash seedlings into the garden.** Wait until a week or so after the last frost date. To minimize transplant shock, plants should be no more than 4 weeks old. It's also warm enough now to begin direct-seeding pumpkins.

■ **Begin transplanting peppers and eggplants into the garden.** Wait until 2 to 3 weeks after the last frost date for these tender plants, until the soil has warmed to 60°F. Like peppers, eggplants belong to the nightshade family. Although most eggplants are blackish purple, they come in a range of shapes and colors. For short-season gardeners, it's best to grow cultivars that mature early, such as 'Millionaire Hybrid' (55 days) or 'Orient Express' (58 days). These are thin, shiny black, Oriental-style eggplants that grow 10 to 12 inches long. For color, you may want to try 'Purple Blush', skinny purple 'Machiaw', or green-and-white variegated 'Kermit', a Thai specialty taking 60 days to mature.

■ **Start fall crops of broccoli, Brussels sprouts, cauliflower, and cabbage by direct seeding or starting flats for transplanting in June and July.** These vegetables all belong to the genus *Brassica*—they're collectively referred to as brassicas—and all require similar growing conditions; they prefer moist, fertile soil high in organic matter. Many brassicas cannot tolerate summer heat, so most gardeners grow them in spring and fall, when the weather is favorably cool. Chinese cabbage thrives throughout the growing season, but it may bolt (go to seed) after a cold snap. To avoid this problem, sow Chinese cabbage near the last frost date.

■ **Set herb transplants into the garden.** It's time to move dill, Greek oregano, sweet marjoram, cilantro, rosemary, sage, summer and winter savory, thyme, and garlic chives to the garden. Be sure to wait until the weather is warm and settled to move basil and lemon grass transplants. Let some dill and cilantro go to seed in the garden, since both annual herbs will self-sow in successive years. Give all these herbs full sun and well-drained soil.

■ **Plant strawberries.** First determine which type of strawberry you want to grow—day-neutral, everbearing, June-bearing, or alpine. Day-neutrals fruit heavily in June and continue into fall. Everbearers also bear heavily in June and produce a second crop of smaller berries up to two months later. June-bearing plants tend to be vigorous, spreading rapidly by runners and producing abundantly in June. Removing the flowers the first year encourages the development of runners. Alpine strawberries are the easiest to grow. Somewhat larger than wild strawberries, these fragrant little fruits appear in summer on compact plants with few to no runners, and continue fruiting into fall.

M a y

JUNE'S TASKS

THE WHOLE GARDEN
- Water newly planted plants and transplants.
- Do the watering early in the morning.
- Weed planting beds as necessary.
- Throw healthy garden clippings onto the compost pile.

TREES AND SHRUBS
- Deadhead rhododendrons, azaleas, mountain laurels, and lilacs.
- Deadhead repeat-blooming roses to encourage more flowers.
- Spray roses early and regularly to prevent fungal diseases.
- Fertilize roses, except for once-blooming roses.
- Continue planting trees, shrubs, ground covers, and other plants purchased in containers.
- Continue pruning conifers such as pines, firs, and spruces.

FLOWERS AND GRASSES
- Sow annual seeds.
- Transplant warm-season annuals on a gray, windless day after the last frost date.
- Stake tall annuals and lax perennials, if you haven't done so already.
- Dig or pull out excess perennials.
- Pinch back chrysanthemums when 4 to 6 inches high.

FRUITS AND VEGETABLES
- Continue direct-seeding vegetable crops.
- Direct-seed or transplant basil when the weather is warm and settled.
- Direct-seed kale, collards, and rutabagas in the garden for fall harvest.
- Finish sowing corn.
- Transplant broccoli, cabbage, cauliflower, and Brussels sprouts starts into the garden for a fall crop.
- Continue transplanting tomatoes, peppers, and eggplants into the garden.
- Continue transplanting or begin direct-seeding pumpkins, summer and winter squash, and melons into the garden.
- Transplant or direct-sow cucumbers into the garden when soil is 70°F.
- Continue transplanting or seeding herbs.

June

Roses, irises, sweet Williams, love-in-a-mist, pinks, and sweet peas—Furber's bouquet and mine parallel each other in glamour, history, and romance. Like Furber, I place *Rosa mundi*, a sport of the ancient apothecary's rose and a traditional cottage garden plant, front and center. First mentioned in Europe in the 16th century, the sweetly fragrant flower has 18 to 24 petals striped deep pink and white. Love-in-a-mist (*Nigella damascena*) is an annual cottage garden favorite with true blue flowers that weave through bolder blooms with ineffable grace and that look as good cut as in the ground. Irises in purple, blue, or maroon form the backbone of my bouquet, while Shasta daisies add country coziness to the arrangement.

Like many cottage garden plants, love-in-a-mist is a self-sowing annual.

I grow the blue 'Miss Jekyll', but Persian Jewels, a popular strain, bears red, pink, purple, and white blooms. Love-in-a-mist's peculiar inflated seedpods look attractive when dried and make a welcome addition to dried arrangements. This annual grows easily in full sun. To help Mother Nature speed the sowing process, remove the seedpods when ripe and crumbly dry, and shake them where you'd like some volunteers to grow. If garden conditions are right, the seeds will produce new plants the following year. Other cottage garden annuals that self-sow include forget-me-nots (*Myosotis sylvatica*), flowering tobacco (*Nicotiana alata*), cosmos (*Cosmos bipinnatus*), pot marigolds (*Calendula officinalis*), and love-lies-bleeding (*Amaranthus caudatus*).

1 Perennial dwarf Sun flower.
Ultramarine & Prusian blew.
Iris Major.
2 Blew Nigella.
or Fennel flower.
3 Moon Trefoile.
4 Upright Sweet William.
5 Saxifrage.
6 Cinque foile.
7
8 Pansies, or Hearts-ease.
9 Maidens blush Rose.
10 Yellow Jasmine.
11 Blew Corn flower.
12 Blush Belgick Roses.
13 The Frankford Roses.
14 Double Martagon.
15 Orchis or Bee flower.
16 Scarlet Colutea.
17 Fraxinella.
18 Moss province Rose.
19 Double Vejonian Silk-grass.
20 White Rose.
21 Dutch Hundred Leav'd Rose.
22 White Batchelors Button.
23 Rosa Mundi.
24 Mountain Lychnis.
25 Dwarf Iris Strip'd.
26 White Jasmine.
27 Scarlet Geranium.
28 Yellow Martagon.
29 Red Martagon.
30 Teucrium or Germander.
31 Mountain dwarf Pinks.
32 Yellow Corn Marygold.
33 Purple Sweet Pea.
34 Greek Valerian.

JUNE

Design'd by P. Casteels.   From the Collection of Rob.t Furber, Gardner at Kensington. 1730.   Engrav'd by H. Fletcher.

June means strawberries—fat, juicy, and ready to pick. The palette of perennials now in bloom is exquisite—pink, white, blue, and silver against a backdrop of fresh grassy green. Among the flowers to enjoy are Shasta daisies, Jacob's ladder (*Polemonium*), magenta cranesbills (*Geranium* spp.), and the starry blue clusters of willow bluestar (*Amsonia tabernaemontana*). Lost in the impossibly sweet fragrance of peonies and old garden roses, I can barely concentrate on work, so lovely is the garden that surrounds me.

THE WHOLE GARDEN

- **Water newly planted plants and transplants.** A deep watering is more beneficial than a light one; moisture that penetrates the soil thoroughly helps the growth of roots buried deep in the ground. Watering lightly encourages the growth of roots at the top of the soil, where they experience acute stress during a drought. Consider placing soaker hoses near plants for maximum water penetration with little runoff.

- **Do the watering early in the morning.** Watering early in the day allows the sun to dry the leaves of your plants, to help ward off the growth of fungal diseases like black spot or powdery mildew on foliage. Avoid watering at midday when the sun is most intense, since a good portion of the water will evaporate before it can help the plant.

- **Weed planting beds as necessary.** Weeds compete with garden plants for soil nutrients, space, and water. Pulling them up promptly helps keep your garden healthy and prevents them from going to seed.

- **Throw healthy garden clippings onto the compost pile.** Discard disease-infected clippings in the trash, to avoid spreading disease-causing organisms in finished compost.

June

GROUNDHOGS

My favorite episode of the television cartoon "Rupert the Bear" has our hairy hero making a topiary groundhog out of his father's favorite shrub. Under the auspices of a wizardly inventor, the tiny topiary turns into a blimp-sized woodchuck that terrorizes the countryside, gobbling everything in sight.

Rupert's story is mine. My garden in its tumescent glory holds the seeds of my despair, for the young shoots so succulent and full of life draw

Nº 1.

PLATE II.

groundhogs to me without fail. This year, masses of *Phlox maculata* 'Alpha', daylilies, hollyhocks, and 100 gladioli succumbed. The miracle is that any garden survived at all. In fact, it surprised me with late-season blooms on early-flowering, groundhog-pruned plants. Thanks to these critters, also called woodchucks, I had non-repeating daylilies that first blossomed in late August and September.

I know I'm not the only woodchuck hater around. Friends of gentle temperament and sophisticated outlook go crazy when the topic turns to woodchucks. I think it has something to do with civilized people losing control of their property and their lives.

Can humans defeat groundhogs? The answer is a qualified *yes*; it takes time and money to succeed. Having watched my husband streak through the backyard in a rainstorm trying to grab one fat critter with a blanket, I was delighted when he decided to electrify his vegetable garden. Little did I realize that the hungry animal, deprived of our produce, would turn with her 4 ravenous babes to my prettiest flower garden for sustenance. I began shouting from windows, attempting to scare the brazen beasts back into the woods.

Aggressive dogs help the problem as long as they patrol outdoors. To fence groundhogs out of a particular garden, erect the fence early in the season—before they know what they're missing inside. Before erecting your fence—to keep them from digging under it—make a trench and line it with chicken wire, then fasten the chicken wire to the above-ground fence. Cages for individual plants, and even floating row covers, also provide effective protection. You can minimize groundhog habitat by eliminating woodpiles and brush piles on your property, but this also eliminates habitat for other wild creatures you may want to attract.

Havahart traps also work, although new groundhogs tend to move in whenever you move an old one out. You need also to be familiar with state laws if you intend to release the animals off your property. (Consider, too, that, according to experts, trapped, relocated animals often do not survive when they are moved into habitats that are already occupied.) And remember to handle the traps carefully, to avoid getting bitten. To entice groundhogs into a trap, first locate an entrance to each of their holes, since they often have more than one in a relatively small area. Set a trap by each, making it irresistible to them: at the back of the trap, toss a couple of fragrant, brown apple cores, torn cabbage leaves, or some old broccoli. Carefully obscure the entrance to the trap with green leaves from nearby plants—last year I used big leaves from a sunflower the groundhogs had toppled—and cover the top of the crate with more leaves and branches so it resembles a natural space. Groundhogs may be smart, but they're also greedy. They'll eventually tread inside to taste the goods and lose the game.

TREES AND SHRUBS

- **Deadhead rhododendrons, azaleas, mountain laurels, and lilacs.** Deadhead these plants after they bloom by snapping off faded flowers. Avoid damaging the buds below the truss, since they are part of the shrub's new growth. Deadheading takes the plant's energy away from setting seed and sends it into leaves and flowers. To keep azaleas bushy, pinch off the stem tips with your fingers soon after flowering. To improve next year's lilac blooms, remove faded flowers at the base within 3 weeks of dying. If you wait until the seeds have begun to form, deadheading will tidy up the shrub's appearance but will not affect next year's flowering.

- **Deadhead repeat-blooming roses to encourage more flowers.** Removing spent flowers from rose bushes keeps them from producing hips or seeds. Setting seed takes up energy that bushes can use to produce more flowers.

- **Spray roses early and regularly to prevent fungal diseases.** Do not spray rugosas, which can be damaged by chemicals. New disease-resistant shrub roses and many old roses generally do not need routine sprays for fungal diseases. Good cultural practices can reduce the need for chemicals: Grow roses suited to your conditions, give them plenty of sunlight and good air circulation. Mulch roses with compost or shredded bark to prevent fungal spores from splashing onto foliage from the ground in rainstorms. Mulching also conserves moisture, which thirsty roses need to grow. Dispose of diseased plant matter in the trash, not the compost pile.

- **Fertilize roses, except for once-blooming roses.** When repeat-flowering roses are finishing their first flush of bloom, apply a high potash fertilizer to stimulate the growth of more flowers.

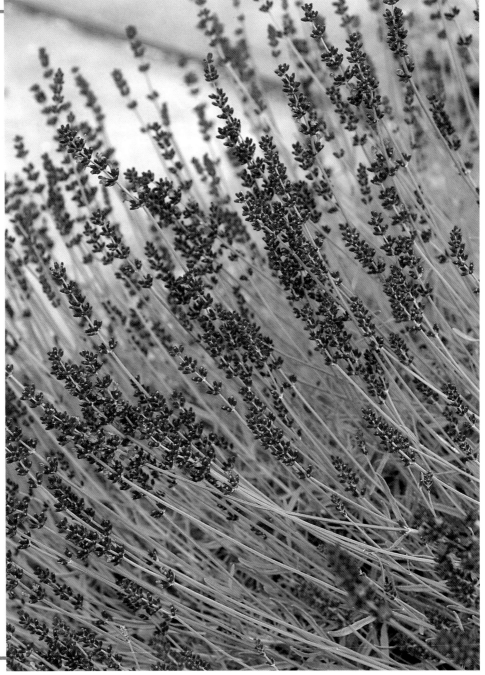

TIP Rose Companions

Once grown nearly exclusively in formal beds with plants lined up in neatly mulched rows, in recent years roses have finally found their way into the garden. Thanks to an abundance of tough, new shrub roses, many of which are disease resistant, these beloved flowers are now great choices for perennial gardens, as well as low-maintenance hedges, shrub borders, and even ground covers. In flower gardens, roses are especially attractive underplanted with low-growing perennials such as lavender, catmints (*Nepeta* spp.), sages (*Salvia* spp.), sundrops (*Oenothera* spp.), and sea kale (*Crambe cordifolia*). Long-blooming annuals, such as petunias or salvias, make good companions as well. Look for cultivars in colors that complement the roses.

Lavandula angustifolia.

FLOWERS AND GRASSES

■ **Sow annual seeds.** Sunflowers, cosmos, zinnias, love-in-a-mist (*Nigella damascena*), and marigolds can be sown directly in the garden if you did not start them earlier indoors.

■ **Transplant warm-season annuals on a gray, windless day after the last frost date.** Moving plants to the garden on a gray or rainy day minimizes stress because it reduces the amount of water lost through leaves.

Nigella damascena.

■ **Stake tall annuals and lax perennials, if you haven't done so already.** It's best to stake dahlias, cannas, and gladioli when you plant them. You can continue planting these flowers up to July 1. Staking early avoids harming the spreading roots later in the season. For taller perennials such as delphiniums, phlox, hollyhocks, or any plant that can't withstand a particularly windy location, it's best to stake before growth has progressed very far. Staking late with a circle-top cage or hoop

creates an unnatural appearance, as the already-mature plant is forced inside the confines of the stake instead of growing naturally through it.

■ **Dig or pull out excess perennials.** False sunflower (*Heliopsis helianthoides*), pink coreopsis (*Coreopsis rosea*), obedient plant (*Physostegia virginiana*), and bee balm (*Monarda* spp.) are examples of perennials that spread fast. Pull up and discard the excess, or dig it for replanting elsewhere; give starts to your neighbors.

■ **Pinch back chrysanthemums when 4 to 6 inches high.** Pinching the stem tips encourages branching and bushy growth, later bloom, and more flower buds.

TIP Hollyhocks Old-fashioned hollyhocks are short-lived perennials best grown as biennials. Give them full sun to light shade, average, well-drained soil, and protection from wind. For the showiest display of blooms, and to minimize problems with the fungal disease rust, start new plants each year. Plant seedlings out in late summer for bloom the following year.

GROWING OLD ROSES

Every garden needs at least one old garden rose, and once you grow one, you'll want to grow more. Tough, vigorous, versatile plants with varied, beautiful flowers, they have a pleasant shrubby habit but can range in size from tiny, 2-foot mounds to ramblers with canes 25 feet or longer.

Old roses are loosely defined as those introduced before 1900. A tighter definition, used by the American Rose Society, holds that old garden roses are those introduced before the appearance of the first hybrid tea rose, 'La France', in 1867. Old garden-rose flowers may be single, five-petaled blooms or very double forms with hundreds of petals piled up and quartered with a perfect button center. Most old garden roses stand out for their perfume—sweet, spicy, citrusy, or as fruity as a ripe apple, depending on the selection. Their often blowsy beauty and

sensual fragrance make them outstanding plants for cutting or to grow near a deck, a patio, or French doors, where you can see and smell them.

Long valued in commercial perfumery, roses also have many uses in cooking and crafts. Dried rosebuds make elegant tabletop topiaries, and the dried petals and buds are treasured ingredients in homemade potpourris. Chefs candy fresh rose petals in sugar and pasteurized or powdered egg white for an edible pastry garnish. They also use rose water in jelly, and in the confection known as Turkish Delight. Herbalists use rose water and rose oil for their soothing effects in lotions, cosmetics, and bath items.

Grow old roses with other roses in mulched beds or plant them in mixed borders with annuals, perennials, and shrubs to complement the roses and extend the season of bloom. The lavish cream, mid-pink, and deep rosy flower spikes of biennial foxgloves (*Digitalis purpurea*), especially the Excelsior Hybrids, look magical near old roses, which typically come in shades of magenta, pink, and white. Silvery artemisias, sages, and lamb's ears, and the green-gray foliage of rue and lavender enhance the colors of old roses but need perfect drainage to survive. Roses and clematis are another happy combination, especially when the clematis can climb over the growing rose canes.

In the North, many old roses are perfectly hardy. Gallicas, albas, damasks, centifolias, and rugosas survive rough winters without complaint to Zone 4, or even 3, depending on the cultivar. Roses grown on their own roots have an added advantage, since they can die back to the ground and, if hardy, come back from the roots the following year.

Apothecary's rose
(*Rosa gallica* var. *officinalis*).

Old garden roses grow readily in a range of ordinary garden soils. Give them full sun—at least 6 hours a day. While they need plenty of water to grow well, roses also need good drainage, since they can't survive wet feet for long. To conserve moisture and cool their roots, treat them to annual mulching with compost or well-aged manure topped off with shredded bark in the spring before they bloom. (Keep the mulch a few inches away from the canes of the plants.) They'll reward you with a period of abundant flowers and continued healthy growth.

Most old garden roses bloom once a year in early summer. In the eastern United States where Japanese beetles ravish roses in bloom, once-blooming types are mostly finished by early July, right before the hungry beetles attack. Old roses also need little pruning: Remove dead, diseased, damaged, crossed, or rubbing canes in early spring. To reduce the size of an overgrown bush, cut back the canes by about a third, making cuts at a 45-degree angle just above an outward-facing bud. Otherwise, let the plants grow naturally, since their shrubby habit fits in well with relaxed, contemporary landscapes.

As there are literally hundreds of old roses to choose from, deciding which ones to grow can be a daunting task. For starters, I've listed 5 favorites below.

Rosa rugosa var. *alba*. A sport of rugosa rose (*R. rugosa*), this 4-foot spreading shrub bears clove-scented, single white flowers. It is a repeat bloomer introduced in 1845. Orange hips follow the flowers.

Rosa gallica var. *officinalis*. Apothecary's rose is a once-blooming rose from ancient Persia used medicinally in the Middle Ages. It features deep pink, semidouble flowers on a spreading, 3- to 4-foot shrub.

Rosa gallica 'Tuscany'. This once-blooming, 4-foot shrub rose is an ancient gallica rose with dark crimson, semidouble flowers that have a boss of bright gold stamens in the center.

Rosa × *centifolia* 'Old Pink Moss'. This cultivar of cabbage rose, introduced before 1700, is grown for its double, intensely fragrant pink flowers and the unusual bristlelike growths, called moss, that cover the sepals and stems. Once-blooming for up to two months, it is also sold as 'Common Moss', 'Muscosa', and 'Communis'.

Rosa alba 'Queen of Denmark'. A once-blooming, 6-foot shrub, this alba rose bears medium pink, very double blooms that have a powerful fragrance, about 200 petals, and a button center. It was introduced in 1826.

Rosa alba 'Queen of Denmark', also known as 'Königin von Dänemark'.

■ **Continue direct-seeding vegetable crops.** Many vegetables —including beans, beets, endive, escarole, fennel, okra, parsley, carrots, radishes, Swiss chard, turnips, and lettuce—can be sown right in the garden once the weather is warm enough. Harvest lettuce leaves 2 to 3 times before the plant goes to seed. For carrots, consider growing round little 'Thumbelina', a 1992 All-America winner that's ready to harvest in just 50 days. It has a short top and a diameter of only 1 to 1½ inches. Sow carrots again in 3 weeks to harvest over a longer period of time. Dig carrots after they've turned bright orange.

■ **Direct-seed or transplant basil when the weather is warm and settled.** Basil is one of the easiest herbs to grow and one of the most satisfying to use in salads, pestos, soups, and stews. Don't rush to move transplants of this cold-sensitive herb to the garden, though. Although many flavored cultivars are available, I like the intensity and fragrance of 'Genovese'. If you give your basil plenty of water and harvest it to prevent flowering, you can grow bushy 24- to 30-inch-tall plants that produce fresh new leaves for weeks.

■ **Direct-seed kale, collards, and rutabagas in the garden for fall harvest.** Fast, steady growth is the secret to success with kale and collards, so give them rich, evenly moist soil and cool temperatures. Rutabagas make tasty additions to fall and winter soups and stews, and grow best in deeply prepared rich soil. Thin plants to 8 inches and mulch the soil with compost to keep it cool and moist.

■ **Transplant broccoli, cabbage, cauliflower and Brussels sprouts starts into the garden for a fall crop.** All can also be direct-sown. For best results, sow 3 or 4 seeds every foot, then thin to the one healthiest seedling in each group.

■ **Continue transplanting tomatoes, peppers, and eggplants into the garden.** There's no harm in waiting to get transplants of these cold-sensitive crops into the garden. In fact, sturdy plants that haven't been stressed by exposure to cold often out-perform ones moved to the garden before the weather is sufficiently warm. Tomato transplants should be 6 weeks old when you transplant them.

■ **Continue transplanting or begin direct-seeding pumpkins, summer and winter squash, and melons into the garden.** 'Rocket', a sturdy pumpkin growing to 12 to 20 pounds, stands out for its ability to stay rot-free all fall. (I displayed 14 of them on my front steps from mid-September through November 30 and only one developed a small black spot before we discarded them.)

■ **Transplant or direct-sow cucumbers into the garden when soil is 70°F.** Wait at least a week after the last frost to transplant; wait longer in a cold, wet spring. Cucumbers need plenty of space to grow so set the transplants 2 feet apart and the rows 5 feet apart.

GARDEN-FRESH HERBS

As every gardener and cook knows, herbs picked fresh from the garden add rich flavor to many foods. However, not every herb will impart the flavor you expect. Tarragon and oregano are two good examples: both are treasured for the pungent fragrance and flavor they add to a variety of dishes, but not all plants of these two popular herbs are created equal. Two kinds of tarragon are widely sold, but only one is good for cooking. French tarragon (*Artemisia dracunculus* var. *sativa*) is a key ingredient in *fines herbes*, a French herbal blend that also includes thyme, parsley, and chervil and is used by chefs in egg dishes and for sauces. For extra flavor, some cooks add a sprig of French tarragon to the bay, thyme, and parsley in *bouquet garni*, another French blend of herbs and spices. *Bouquet garni* is typically tied up in cheesecloth so it can be added to soups, sauces, and stews and easily removed before serving.

Russian tarragon (*A. dracunculus* ssp. *dracunculoides*), on the other hand, has no taste at all. Although nurseries sell it along with other herbs—sometimes simply, and misleadingly, labeled "tarragon"—it has no culinary value whatsoever. In fact, it looks and acts like a weed in the garden. You'll rue the day you planted it, since it spreads ferociously when given a chance. Russian tarragon is easily propagated from seed, whereas true French tarragon must be propagated by cuttings or division, since its seeds are sterile. Buy French tarragon only from a reputable nursery. It's best to taste before you buy: If you rub a narrow leaf of fresh French tarragon in your fingers, you'll notice a sharp aniselike fragrance and flavor, which the leaves of Russian tarragon plants will lack. Both French and

the right variety to grow, because some garden centers and catalogues offer several kinds. *Origanum vulgare* ssp. *vulgare*, also listed as *O. vulgare*, is a tasteless plant but looks attractive and shrubby in the garden. For the pungent culinary oregano rich with essential oils, buy seeds—or better yet plants—of Greek oregano (*O. vulgare* ssp. *hirtum* or *O. heracleoticum*), which is hardy to

Russian tarragon are hardy to Zone 3. Texas tarragon, or Mexican mint marigold (*Tagetes lucida*), hardy to Zone 8, has an anisey fragrance that makes it an effective replacement for French tarragon in hot climates. It can be grown as an annual in the north.

Oregano, ubiquitous in Italian food, is another popular kitchen herb. Here too, it's important to know

Zone 5. Seed-grown plants will vary in flavor and pungence, so if you start from seeds, rogue out flavorless plants mercilessly. Here, too, if you start with plants, it's a good idea to taste before you buy. Sweet marjoram (*O. majorana*), a tender perennial grown as an annual in the North, has a milder taste than Greek oregano and is hardy only to Zone 9.

Summer

. . . There's no blue quite so blue as the summer sky—perfect, clear, intense. Shimmering heat envelops trees, lawns, shrubs, and flowers. The day lures me. I hear the insects whir before they eat me.

THE WHOLE GARDEN

- Turn the compost pile.
- Keep up with weeds in garden beds.
- Water your garden during periods of drought.

TREES AND SHRUBS

- Deadhead some spring-blooming shrubs.
- Deadhead and feed repeat-blooming roses.
- Prune repeat-blooming climbing roses.
- Use good hygiene for rose health.
- Prune vines that bloom on old wood immediately after blooming.
- Prune birches, cherries, maples, horse chestnuts, lindens, and walnuts once the new growth is fully developed.
- Clip yew hedges and topiaries.
- Remove dead stems, branches, and leaves from trees and shrubs.
- Create beds around trees and shrubs to protect them from lawn mower damage.

FLOWERS AND GRASSES

- Early in the month, finish transplanting annuals into the garden.
- Fertilize container plants regularly.
- Stake tall plants growing in windy sites.
- Pinch back asters, dahlias, cosmos, zinnias, salvias, and chrysanthemums.
- Cut spent perennials to the ground to encourage new growth.
- Deadhead flowers to prolong bloom time.
- Divide and replant bearded iris.
- Divide daylilies that have finished blooming.
- Dig and divide spring-blooming bulbs that flowered sparsely.
- Cut back daffodil leaves after they turn yellow.
- Watch your color scheme develop.

FRUITS AND VEGETABLES

- Continue planting broccoli, cabbage, and cauliflower transplants for fall crops.
- Continue direct-seeding vegetable and herb crops.
- Beginning mid-month, direct-seed vegetables such as spinach for fall crops.
- Harvest onions and garlic after the tops start to yellow and die back.
- Harvest and dry herbs for the winter.
- Give your vegetable garden at least 1 inch of water per week during periods of drought.

July

As the season waxes to its fullest, an abundance of flowers is blooming in the garden, making it a cinch to create a stunning bouquet. Furber harvested lilies, lupines, valerian, marigolds, stock, larkspur, lychnis, and honeysuckle for his arrangement, but I heed my own whim and cut gooseneck loosestrife (*Lysimachia clethroides*), pink and white spider flowers (*Cleome hasslerana*), trusses of pink butterfly bush (*Buddleia davidii* 'Pink Delight'), and an assortment of *Monarda*, better known as bee balm. Though they have a reputation for looking stiff and funereal, I also add the vertical stalks and ruffled flowers of gladiolus to formal bouquets, where they lend a charming air of Victorian stateliness.

Bee balm—a perennial herb bearing lacy clusters of tubular flowers that explode at the tips of 3- to 4-foot-tall stems—attracts hummingbirds, a boon to any garden. Among the excellent, mildew-resistant cultivars are pink 'Marshall's Delight', 'Gardenview Scarlet', and deep violet-purple 'Prairie Night'. Other herbs with flowers suitable for arrangements include basil (*Ocimum basilicum*), anise hyssop (*Agastache foeniculum*), lavender (*Lavandula* spp.), rosemary (*Rosmarinus officinalis*), and purple coneflower (*Echinacea purpurea*). Although the purple rays, or petals, of coneflowers don't last long once cut, the prickly, hedgehog-like cones they surround make a striking, everlasting addition to both fresh and dried bouquets.

Common sage (*Salvia officinalis*), a woody perennial, comes in many foliage colors and bears two-lipped bluish-purple flowers that attract bees. Its leaves have a spicy, earthy fragrance and long, graceful stems. The species leaves are gray-green and downy to the touch, while the cultivar 'Tricolor' bears crinkled, irregularly variegated leaves marked in creamy white, rosy purple, and soft gray-green. Pineapple sage (*S. elegans*) is a tender perennial with bright red flowers; its foliage has a distinct pineapple fragrance. Clary sage (*S. sclarea*), an upright biennial, bears striking purple and white flowers with ornamental purple bracts.

1 Double Nasturtium.
2 Double white Maudlin.
3 Prince picoté July flower.
4 True Caper.
5 Virginian yellow Jasmine.
6 Painted Lady Carnation.
7 Double blew Throat-wort.
8 Scarlet Martagon.
9 White Lilly strip'd with purple
10 Spanish Broom.
11 Carolina kidney bean tree.
12 Double strip't female balsam.
13 True Olive tree.
14 Red Oleander.
15 Painted Lady pink.
16 White Lupin.

JULY

27 Prince's picoté July flower.
28 Geranium noctu olens.
29 White Valerian.
20 Hoop Horn beam.
21 Indian or china pink.
22 Double Pomegranate.
23 Double mouse ear.
24 Virginian scarlet honey suckle.
25 Double white Throat-wort.
26 French Marigold.
28 Double scarlet Lychnis.
29 Double blew Larkspur.
29 Hungarian Climer.
30 Double Stock.
31 Bean Caper.
32 White Oleander.

Design'd by Pdr Casteels.

From the Collection of Robt Furber Gardner at Kensington 1730.

Engrav'd by H. Fletcher.

In the garden, the sun grows hot, the plants big, the flowers and herbs profuse. Strong sunlight makes bold blues, intense yellows, glowing oranges, deep pinks, and rich purples shine by day. At night, white flowering tobacco shimmers in moonlight and perfumes the air with spice. I give bags of basil to a local pizza shop. Weeds proliferate, much like the groundhogs that ate 99 of my gladiolus corms, leaving me one stalk of pristine white flowers to bring indoors. Four groundhogs visited my Havahart trap this month, along with a possum, which fooled me by playing . . . possum.

THE WHOLE GARDEN

■ **Turn the compost pile.** Organisms hard at work in your compost pile need air to break down garden clippings and kitchen refuse. Turning a pile aerates it, hastening the decay and ultimate breakdown of composted materials. To turn your pile, use a garden or compost fork and simply move the contents from the existing pile to a new one right next to it. Balancing "wet and green, brown and dry" is the secret, albeit a somewhat cryptic one, to a successful compost pile. Combining these two types of compostables ensures relatively quick breakdown. Add "wet and green" materials— fresh grass, kitchen scraps (but no meat or fish), green weeds, succulent leaves— if the ingredients in your pile don't seem to be breaking down. Add "brown and dry" materials— shredded paper, sawdust, dry grass, dry leaves—if your pile is slimy or smelly. Rotted manure violates this simple rule: Use it as you would "wet and green" materials, since it speeds decomposition of "brown and dry" materials.

■ **Keep up with weeds in garden beds.** In warm weather, weeds can quickly overtake garden beds, competing with your precious plants for space and vital nutrients. To keep them under control, weed regularly and thoroughly. If you weed after a rain it will be easier to pull them up roots and all—an important consideration since many perennials can come back from just a fragment of root left in the soil. If you don't have time to weed, at least pull off weed flowers whenever they appear and discard them in the trash—not the compost—so they don't set seeds.

■ **Water the garden during periods of drought.** Plants most vulnerable to the effects of drought include seedlings, young plants, and recent transplants, so make every effort to keep them watered until they are well established. Always water deeply—wetting more than the top couple inches of soil—to encourage deep roots and and tolerance to drought.

TREES AND SHRUBS

■ **Deadhead some spring-blooming shrubs.** While shrubs that bloom along the length of their stems—bridal wreath is one example—don't benefit from deadheading, some spring-blooming shrubs do. Remove the spent flowers of lilacs and rhododendrons as soon as possible after they fade; either snap the flowers off between thumb and forefinger, or clip them off with pruners right at the base of the truss. Try to do this before seeds have formed—within 3 weeks after the flowers fade—to prevent the plant from spending its energy to set seeds. Deadheading also tidies up the shrub's appearance.

■ **Deadhead and feed repeat-blooming roses.** Deadheading these plants is another summertime chore that pays off: It not only makes plants look more attractive, but cutting off faded flowers encourages new blooms to form. To make sure repeat-blooming roses perform at their peak, feed them once the first flush of flowers has faded. Hybrid teas, multifloras, grandifloras, and some shrub roses all benefit from a dose of a complete rose food spread around the base of each plant according to the label directions.

When deadheading, clip dead blooms to a healthy shoot or an outward-facing bud. On roses with sprays of dead blooms, take the entire spray back to a shoot or a bud.

■ **Prune repeat-blooming climbing roses.** To stimulate more flower buds to form on repeat-blooming climbers, cut back the tips of lateral shoots after the first flush of bloom has passed.

■ **Use good hygiene for rose health.** Clean up pruned twigs and leaves immediately, especially if they show signs of disease. Pick diseased leaves off plants as they appear. Toss infected debris in the trash, not the compost pile.

■ **Prune vines that bloom on old wood immediately after blooming.** This is the time to prune *Wisteria* spp., climbing hydrangea (*Hydrangea petiolaris*), and five-leaf akebia (*Akebia quinata*). Take off shoots that bear faded blossoms and cut back non-blooming stems just above the start of new growth.

■ **Prune birches, cherries, maples, horse chestnuts, lindens, and walnuts once the new growth is fully developed.** These trees produce copious amounts of sap

during their initial growth spurt, in late winter and early spring. By summer, both growth and sap production have slowed, making it safe to prune them.

- **Clip yew hedges and topiaries.** Japanese yew (*Taxus cuspidata*), an excellent choice for topiaries and hedges in Zones 4 to 7, has growth spurts in March and June, so this is the perfect time for its annual pruning. This plant also makes an attractive small evergreen shade tree. Once you train it into a tree shape, with one or more trunks, let it develop a heavy canopy. The shoot tips need light for regrowth, so new shoots will gradually be shaded out at the bottom. As you trim off the dead branches underneath, you'll expose the yew's handsome reddish peeling bark.

- **Remove dead stems, branches, and leaves from trees and shrubs.** Regardless of the season or the plant, prune out dead stems and branches, and, when possible, pick off diseased leaves. Discard diseased and dead plant material in the trash, not the compost pile.

- **Create beds around trees and shrubs to protect them from lawn mower damage.** The easiest way to get rid of grass is to smother it by spreading a layer of newspaper, 6 to 8 sheets thick, topped with shredded bark mulch. Keep the beds mulched until fall, then plant them with spring-flowering bulbs and perennial ground covers. Dig carefully and not too deep to avoid damaging the tree roots. Beds not only protect trunks from being whacked by lawn mowers, but they also make trimming the lawn around trees and shrubs a breeze.

Surrounding trees and shrubs with ground covers—beds of perennials and bulbs—instead of lawngrass is not only attractive, but also makes sense from a maintenance standpoint. Beds make mowing easy, reduce the need to trim, and protect the trunks of trees and shrubs from lawn mower damage.

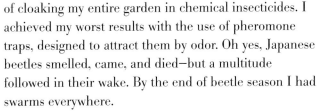

JAPANESE BEETLES

The sight of iridescent Japanese beetles—inhabiting the crevice between two rose petals, or pairing off on partially chewed leaves—brings out the worst in me. I want to squeeze them, pound them, snip them in two—anything to preserve my roses. Actually, it's not just roses they devour—cinquefoils (*Potentilla* spp.), false sunflowers (*Heliopsis* spp.), and Harry Lauder's walking stick (*Corylus avellana* 'Contorta') are just a few of the many plants Japanese beetles consume with relish.

I've tried just about everything to destroy Japanese beetles, which haunt states east of the Mississippi, short of cloaking my entire garden in chemical insecticides. I achieved my worst results with the use of pheromone traps, designed to attract them by odor. Oh yes, Japanese beetles smelled, came, and died—but a multitude followed in their wake. By the end of beetle season I had swarms everywhere.

My neighbor, who owns a lawn-care company, advised me that if I wanted to improve the beetle situation, I had to get rid of my roses. Of course I could never do that, because, to paraphrase the Little Prince, it's the time I spend on my roses that makes them so dear to me. I did, however, beat those bugs at their own game by replacing my fragrant repeat-bloomers

(goodbye, 'Columbus') with once-blooming old garden roses. My old-fashioned roses bloom lavishly in June, but by the time the beetles arrive in July, they're finished for the season.

There are a few fragrant, repeat-blooming roses that I refuse to give up: 'Abraham Darby', 'Brother Cadfael', *Rosa rugosa* var. *alba*, and 'Carefree Beauty' are all visited by Japanese beetles in my garden. To keep beetles under control, on my daily garden excursion I carry a big plastic cup filled with water and a squirt of dishwashing liquid. I hold the cup under infested leaves and flowers and gently shake those critters into the soapy liquid, where they drown. I also plant some repeat-blooming roses that have little or no fragrance. The climber 'Blaze', and ground-cover roses such as 'Baby Blanket' and 'Seafoam' look great, and in my garden they seem to be immune to beetle attack.

Each year I donate my Harry Lauder's walking stick to the beetles, and let them enjoy it undisturbed. By mid-August, when it's bare of leaves, I think of how my gift prevented those voracious insects from eating other plants. I've also found that controlling the beetle grubs in the grass not only helps the lawn stay attractive (the grubs eat grass roots), but it also cuts down on the number of beetles that will eventually emerge. Treating the lawn for grubs with organic remedies such as milky spore disease—a bacteria that kills them and that will persist in the soil for several years—works best if you convince as many of your neighbors as you can to follow suit.

Other methods of controlling beetles include spraying infested plants with neem, a botanical insecticide that is biodegradable and fairly nontoxic to pets and wildlife. You can also encourage some natural predators of Japanese beetles to visit your garden. Attract parasitic wasps and flies to your garden with plants rich in pollen and nectar—daisies, asters, mints, dill, and catnip are good choices—and you're bound to reduce the number of beetles on your plants.

FLOWERS AND GRASSES

■ **Early in the month, finish transplanting annuals into the garden.** It's still not too late to add annuals and frost-tender perennials to the garden, including geraniums (*Pelargonium* spp.), tuberous begonias, and heliotrope (*Heliotropium arborescens*). Transplant on a cloudy, windless day when the soil is damp. Moving plants on a hot, sunny, windy day can dry out plant roots and inhibit growth.

*Garden*Magic

INSTALL A NEW LAWN

While it's true that July isn't the best time to sow grass seeds, this isn't as crazy a suggestion as it sounds. If you're planning to install a new lawn in September, now's the time to prepare the soil. Start the process in mid to late July by plowing under your existing lawn. Remove as many rocks as possible either by hand or, in very stony soil, with a specialized tool such as a mechanical rock hound. Do a soil test to determine which amendments you will need for a healthy lawn—perhaps lime to adjust the pH, fertilizer for nutrients, or compost to increase organic matter.

Rake the amended soil to prepare it for seeding. Water the earth and let it lie fallow for two to three weeks to encourage weeds to germinate. Chop down the emerging weed seedlings with a hoe, or spray them with a non-residual herbicide. Repeat the water-wait-spray cycle twice more, at three-week intervals.

Before sowing, spread a starter fertilizer on the soil, unless you are planning on hydroseeding. (Hydroseed is a slurry of grass seeds, water-absorbing granules, and organic matter such as straw that can be sprayed on sites by a contractor.) Check with your local Cooperative

Extension Service for the best grass seed or seed blends for your specific area and conditions. Don't make the mistake of buying cheap seed; new cultivars with improved disease and insect resistance, as well as drought tolerance, are available and well worth the cost. Cheap seed blends also often contain a larger quantity of weed seeds than more expensive brands.

Sow seed in early September in Zone 5. Pay close attention to the seeding rate (the number of seeds per thousand square feet); this rate depends on the type of seed you select, because different grass species differ significantly in the weight per seed. For instance, tall fescues have approximately 375,000 seeds per pound, whereas Kentucky bluegrass has 2,400,000 seeds per pound, or 6 times more seeds per pound than tall fescues. Thus it takes 8 pounds of tall fescue seed to cover 1,000 square feet, versus only 3 pounds of Kentucky bluegrass seed for the same area.

After spreading seeds, use a roller to ensure good seed-to-soil contact. Keep the lawn constantly moist for 2 weeks, until grass seedlings appear.

■ **Fertilize container plants regularly.** Use a diluted liquid fertilizer every 2 weeks to keep plants growing vigorously. Or apply slow-release granules according to package directions.

■ **Stake tall plants growing in windy sites.** If you didn't stake your tall annuals and perennials early, do it now, but take care not to damage their roots or stems when installing the supports. Inexpensive bamboo stakes pushed deeply into the ground and string or twine are enough to keep plants in place. Stake each of the main shoots for maximum support. If you installed your stakes early in the season, you may need to install taller ones as the plants grow.

■ **Pinch back asters, dahlias, cosmos, zinnias, salvias, and chrysanthemums.** Pinching off the growing tips between your thumb and forefinger encourages the development of side shoots and/or flower buds, bushier plants, and often denser flower clusters; it also delays bloom. Don't pinch chrysanthemums later than July 4th, or you may sacrifice fall flowers.

Pinching stems' tips yields compact mums with abundant flowers.

Digging In

Containers filled with flowers and foliage look attractive nearly anywhere in the garden. Use them to dress up a patio, terrace, or deck, or to add brilliant summer-long color in constricted spaces like porches and balconies. Containers also make excellent focal points for converging garden paths, and can be used to mark a garden's entrances and exits. To look good all summer long, however, potted plants require special care.

You can grow plants in all manner of containers, including conventional pots, half-barrels with holes drilled in the bottom, window boxes, and even old shoes, buckets, or other flea market finds. Whatever you choose, containers must have drainage holes. Fill them with a commercial potting soil to within 1 or 2 inches of the rim. Since commercial mixes, especially those that contain composted bark, can be difficult to wet, it's a

good idea to premoisten them by putting the mix in a 5-gallon bucket or other large container and stirring in water. To help prevent soil from spilling out of a pot's bottom hole, lay a small piece of landscape fabric or even an air conditioner filter on the drainage material before pouring soil. This fabric will also help contain the roots of the plant.

Fill containers with one type of plant—marigolds or impatiens, for example—or try mixing a variety of different species to create a "micro-garden." Include flowers or foliage plants that will trail over the edges, and plan on an attractive mix of shapes, sizes, and textures, as well as colors. Be sure to combine plants that require basically the same growing conditions; mixing plants that need sun with those that prefer shade in a single container is a recipe for disappointing results.

Container-grown plants need to be watered regularly all summer long. Because they usually don't hold much soil, containers dry out quickly. Ones situated in a windy spot or on a hot deck or patio are especially prone to drying out. In addition, water evaporates more quickly from containers made of porous materials, such as terra-cotta or wood, than from non-porous plastic or fiberglass. You need to check the soil's moisture content daily—and, during the dog days of summer, twice a day—to see if the soil needs watering. The addition of water-storing polymer crystals to the soil mix will increase the amount of moisture retained in the pot. (For example, Gardener's Supply Company sells HydroSource, a water-absorbent polymer in both coarse and fine grinds, and HydroSoil, a soil mix that includes these crystals along with peat, perlite, and vermiculite for aeration. Similarly, Burpee sells Terra Sorb, another water-storing material.)

Frequent watering means frequent fertilization, since nutrients are washed from the soil each time you water your containerized plants. If you potted your plants in a commercial potting soil that includes fertilizer, then you won't have to fertilize for the first 8 to 10 weeks. After that, you need to apply fertilizer every 2 to 3 weeks according to the directions on the fertilizer package. For less frequent applications, apply a slow-release fertilizer to the soil surface.

■ **Cut spent perennials to the ground to encourage new growth.** To encourage healthy new leaves and fuller plants, whack to the ground those spring-blooming perennials that are past their prime. Slug-eaten lungworts (*Pulmonaria* spp.), leggy spiderworts (*Tradescantia* spp.), and floppy mountain bluets (*Centaurea montana*) all respond to this harsh treatment with new growth if you water them deeply and perhaps feed them with a shovelful of compost. Try it with scraggly pansies or Johnny-jump-ups (*Viola* spp.), too.

■ **Deadhead flowers to prolong bloom time.** Regular deadheading keeps gardens looking neat, and if you take the time to remove spent blossoms before the plant begins to set seed, many annuals will bloom longer. Cutting back perennials such as coreopsis, lavender, and delphinium after their first flowering also encourages a second flush of bloom.

To keep bearded irises blooming abundantly for years to come, divide plants in midsummer every four years. Clumps bloom sparsely the following spring but regain their splendor the year after that.

■ **Divide and replant bearded iris.** Bearded irises need dividing about every 4 years to keep them vigorous. The best time to divide is after blooming, when new roots start to grow. Bearded irises grow from clumps of thick, branching, underground stems called rhizomes. To divide them, lift the clump with a garden fork, taking care not to dig too close to the plant's base or damage the roots that grow from the rhizomes; the more intact roots left on each rhizome, the more quickly the new plant will reestablish itself. Brush off excess dirt, and pull the clump apart with your hands. Throw away the oldest rhizomes and any that are soft or damaged. Using a clean, sharp knife, cut pieces of fleshy young rhizomes from the clump. Cut off ⅓ of the longest roots and trim the fan of leaves on

each rhizome to 6 inches. Then replant the rhizomes about 6 inches apart, setting each one about halfway *above* ground. Be sure to select a sunny location in well-drained garden soil.

■ **Divide daylilies that have finished blooming.** While some daylilies bloom for years without dividing, many of the newer hybrids form such dense, vigorous clumps that they need dividing every 3 to 4 years to keep them blooming at their peak. To divide, dig the clumps with a fork or sharp spade, cut the foliage back to about 3 inches, and brush off excess soil. To separate the dense mass of fleshy and fibrous roots, either insert 2 garden forks back-to-back in the clump and pull them gently apart, or use your hands or a sharp, clean knife to separate sections of the plant. Divisions with 3 or 4 "fans" of leaves are ideal. Replant immediately, or pot up divisions to share with fellow gardeners. Be sure to discard any plant parts that look diseased or damaged.

If daylily clumps bloom sparsely, it's time to dig and divide. Newly divided clumps won't bloom well the first year, but will repay your efforts in subsequent years.

■ **Dig and divide spring-blooming bulbs that flowered sparsely.** Sparse bloom indicates these plants are overcrowded. To divide, dig up clumps with a garden fork, brush off excess dirt, then separate the individual bulbs. Clean them gently, removing faded leaves and loose, flaky pieces of their brown skin. Throw away bulbs that look sick, rotted, or damaged. It's easiest to replant them immediately, but

you also can arrange the bulbs on a rack so they don't touch and let them dry for several hours. Then dust with sulfur, an organic fungicide, and store them in a dark, dry, warm place, in paper or net bags, until fall planting time.

■ **Cut back daffodil leaves after they turn yellow.** The ripening leaves of spring bulbs such as daffodils may be unattractive, but they're essential because they

make food to fuel next year's flowers. Never tie, rubber band, or braid yellowing daffodil leaves either, however ugly they may be, because this practice results in lowered plant vitality. Once leaves have turned completely yellow, remove them by either pulling them up or cutting them off, then scuff some dirt or mulch over the foliage hole in the ground to discourage narcissus bulb flies, which can infest old bulb clumps. If you see a yellow-and-brown fly with one pair of wings entering a bulb hole, dig up affected bulbs and discard them to prevent the infestation from spreading.

■ **Watch your color scheme develop.** My island flower bed glows pink and blue in June, but in July the color scheme depends on the contrast between deep golden false sunflower *Heliopsis helianthoides* 'Karat' and the blackish purple flowers of hollyhock *Alcea rosea* 'Nigra'. Note how your garden evolves during the growing season and how you can improve it by adding, subtracting, or rearranging elements of color.

FRUITS AND VEGETABLES

■ **Continue direct-seeding vegetable and herb crops.** Fennel, Swiss chard, turnips, beans, endive, escarole, and lettuce are some of the vegetables you can continue planting every 2 or 3 weeks to ensure a continuous harvest. Herbs to sow include basil, cutting celery, dill, cilantro, sweet marjoram, summer savory, and parsley.

■ **Beginning mid-month, direct seed vegetables such as spinach for fall crops.** Begin sowing spinach, peas, carrots, and

TURNIP

SEVEN TOP

CARD SEED. CO.
FREDONIA, N.Y.

rutabagas for fall and winter use. Because spinach seeds germinate best in cool soil, seeds sown in midsummer's warm soil will have a lower rate of germination. Sow seeds in a row ½ inch deep and 1 to 2 inches apart. Keep the soil evenly moist to discourage plants from going to seed. Peas need a sunny location with good air circulation and light, well-drained, fairly fertile soil to thrive. Choose mildew-resistant cultivars like 'Oregon Giant' snow peas or 'Knight', 'Maestro', and 'Bounty'

garden (shelling) peas for fall harvest. For a fall crop of beets to store through the winter, sow 10 weeks before the first heavy freeze in fall.

■ **Harvest onions and garlic after the tops start to yellow and die back.** To cure onions, spread the bulbs in the sun in a single layer, on a screen raised off the ground, for at least a week. When they're dry, cut the tops, keeping an inch-long stem. Store the bulbs in onion bags under cool, dry conditions. When harvesting garlic, be careful

not to bruise it, since bruised cloves rot quicky. To cure garlic, hang it by the bunch until dry (2 to 3 weeks) in a warm dry place out of the sun.

■ **Give your vegetable garden at least 1 inch of water per week during periods of drought.** Many vegetables are sweetest and best-tasting when they are grown quickly and evenly. Leafy crops such as lettuce are especially sensitive to dry soil, and will develop bitter-tasting leaves or set seed prematurely as a result.

TIP: Try an Edible Edging Begonias, sweet alyssum, or other low-growing annuals are often used to edge flower beds, but for something a bit different why not try an edging plant with a twist? Spinach is a handsome plant that makes a surprisingly effective edging; just be sure to plant extra in your vegetable garden, because you may decide it's too pretty to pick. Lettuce—especially colorful or frilly-foliaged leaf varieties—is attractive as an edging plant as well. When you are starting seeds for fall crops of these plants, sow some extras to add an edible edging to a flowerbed. For best results, move them into place after cooler fall temperatures arrive. Both also are effective edgings for spring and early-summer plantings.

DRYING HERBS

When your garden is filled with herbs growing so quickly you can't keep up with them, it isn't a problem: it's an opportunity. Snipping sprigs of fresh herbs is a summertime luxury, but taking time to harvest in quantity now—before they've gone to seed, gotten weedy, or become hopelessly overgrown—means you'll be able to enjoy their fragrance and flavor all through the winter months, too. Timely harvesting, when herbs are at their peak of flavor and fragrance, not only keeps plants attractive and healthy, but it also maximizes productivity. Perennial herbs like thyme and rosemary respond to regular harvesting by growing more stems. Harvesting stems and leaves from annuals like basil encourages bushy growth and helps prolong the plant's life by keeping it from flowering and going to seed.

Most herbs owe their taste to volatile oils. To maximize the flavor of the herbs you pick, harvest them when the oils are most pungent. That's usually just before they flower, when the plant is in bud. The flavor also tends to be stronger in the morning, so gather your herbs after the morning dew has dried, but before bright sunlight weakens their potency.

To dry herbs, lay sprigs or large single leaves on a raised screen or wire rack in a dark, dry room. You can also air-dry herbs by hanging them upside-down in small bunches. The drying space should be well-ventilated to keep mold from developing on the cut leaves and stems; darkness can help preserve the herb's original color. Herbs with woody stems like thyme, sage, lavender, and rosemary dry well in bunches tied with string or rubber bands. Depending on the plant and the conditions in the drying room, herbs can take from 1 to 3 weeks to air dry. Dried bunches of herbs and everlasting flowers can make an attractive, rustic addition to your kitchen decor. Exposed to long periods of light and air, however, they'll eventually lose their color, flavor, and fragrance.

Drying herbs in a microwave is quicker, but somewhat riskier, than air-drying them. Herbs crisp quickly in a microwave, but woe to the gardener who microwaves an aromatic herb too long. I once overcooked sage, and its fragrant aroma turned foul, stinking up my kitchen for hours. To microwave herbs, place a single layer of clean, dry sprigs or leaves between paper towels and heat on High for one minute. If further drying is needed, continue in 15-second increments, checking them each time to see if they're ready.

A slower method for drying herbs is in a conventional oven. In a gas oven, the heat from the pilot light is enough to dry herbs arranged in a single layer on a cookie sheet over a 3- to 6-hour period. Keep electric ovens set to 150°F or less and leave the oven door open while drying. Start checking the herbs after 2 to 3 hours and remove them as soon as they feel crisp.

Basil is one popular herb that doesn't dry well. For tips on preserving this kitchen staple, turn to page 119.

AUGUST'S TASKS

THE WHOLE GARDEN
- Collect seeds for next year's garden.
- Continue weeding garden beds.
- Continue watering your garden as needed during dry weather.
- Check plants for signs of pests and diseases.
- Evaluate your garden with an eye for improvements.
- Study bulb catalogues and order garlic and flowering bulbs and corms to plant this fall.

TREES AND SHRUBS
- Train wayward vines.
- Stop pruning shrubs and trees.
- Don't fertilize shrubs and trees after mid-month.
- Consider adding shrubs to flower borders.

FLOWERS AND GRASSES
- Make sure lawns that are not dormant receive 1 inch of water a week.
- Continue deadheading spent flowers to prolong bloom time.
- Cut hollyhocks near the ground after they bloom.
- Divide or transplant Oriental poppies.
- Add extra fall-blooming perennials to the garden.
- Sow self-sowing annuals where you'd like them to appear next spring and summer.
- Cut flowers to bring indoors.
- Continue dividing bearded irises.
- Plant crown imperial (*Fritillaria imperialis*).
- Plant fall crocuses and colchicums as soon as bulbs are available.

FRUITS AND VEGETABLES
- Continue sowing spinach, radishes, endive, escarole, and lettuce for fall crops.
- Direct-seed turnips for a fall harvest.
- Continue harvesting herbs.
- Harvest green lima beans.
- Harvest cucumbers, eggplants, and peppers as they ripen so new ones can develop.
- Propagate strawberries or weed them and thin out the runners.
- Prune away berry canes that have finished fruiting.

August's bouquet has infinite variety in color and form. Among Furber's flowers are many that thrive in American gardens. Passionflower's (*Passiflora* spp.) intricacy of line is irresistible, while cockscomb's (*Celosia cristata*) unique texture begs for a touch. Hollyhock (*Alcea rosea*) has old-fashioned charm, and Turk's-cap lily (*Lilium martagon*) looks elegant potted, cut, or out in a garden bed or border.

To these flowers I add zinnias and sunflowers. Their blooms range from green and yellow to shades of orange, pink, red, and white. A blue ceramic pitcher of sunflowers is a classic of American country style, and a crock of colorful zinnias looks just as delightful in a casual rustic setting. Another fine plant for both gardens and bouquets is great coneflower (*Rudbeckia maxima*). This native, 5- to 6-foot-tall wildflower adds architectural structure to beds, borders, and sunny wild gardens. The plants produce a clump of blue-green leaves up to 18 inches long that are handsome in their own right. Strong, erect flower stems emerge from the clump, and

ust

are topped by daisylike flowers with pointed cones about 2 inches long that stand above drooping yellow rays. The flowers add welcome height to an arrangement of cut flowers, and the dried cones work well in fall and winter bouquets. If you leave great coneflower uncut in the garden, its stems and cones will persist through winter for a striking effect and attract seed-eating birds.

While Furber chooses a Turks-cap lily for his August bouquet, I'll take an Oriental hybrid. Turks-caps are versatile—they're hardy to Zone 3 and tolerate full sun, partial shade, and acid to slightly alkaline soil—but most finish blooming in midsummer. Oriental hybrids, on the other hand, bloom in July and August, carrying lavishly fragrant flowers in shades of white, pink, and red. The ever-popular 'Stargazer' bears deep pink, upturned, perfumed flowers edged in white. 'Stargazer' is acclaimed as a cut or potted bloom, but I like 'Black Beauty' for its sturdy constitution and stunning recurved dark crimson flowers.

1 Purple Althæa frutex.	9 Purple Coxcomb Amaranth.	17 Egyptian scarlet holly hock. 26 Tisole from Genoa.
2 Ivy leav'd Jasmine.	10 Shrub S.t Johns wort.	18 Yellow strip'd marvel of peru. 27 Double spanish Jasmine.
3 Iris Uvaria.	11 Ponds blew Throatwort.	19 Strip'd Monthly rose. 28 White, Eternal.
4 Purple Sultan.	12 Palma Christi.	20 Double fether few. 29 Fruit bearing Passion flower.
5 Purple toad flax.	13 Purple Convolvulus.	21 Semper Augustus Auricula. 30 Scarlet Althæa.
6 Purple Amaranthoides.	14 Purple Convolvulus.	22 Dwarf Convolvulus. 31 Canary shrub fox glove.
7 Double Arabian Jasmine.	15 Indian yellow Jasmine.	23 Willow leav'd Apocynum. 32 Long blowing honey suckle.
8 Yellow Kelmia.	16 Double flowering Myrtle.	24 Guns of America. 33 Double purple Virgins bower.
		25 Virginian flowering Raspberry. 34 Virginian scarlet Martagon.

AUGUST

Design'd by P.r Casteels. From the Collection of Rob.t Furber Gardiner at Kensington 1730. Engrav'd by H. Fletcher.

August's golden light slants across the garden, casting a primeval veil over all the growing things. Weeds and wildflowers battle coddled hybrid blooms. Purple loosestrife, promiscuous and despised, seeds itself into rich damp garden soil. Goldenrod and milkweed come uninvited, along with Queen Anne's lace. Nights grow cooler, and the hottest days are gone until next year. My vegetable garden is in full production now, and I'm harvesting squash, tomatoes, hot peppers, cucumbers, and plenty of herbs. I cut sprigs from a 15-foot row of spice-scented basil twice a week, to keep the plants bushy and free of the flowers that would reduce its productivity.

THE WHOLE GARDEN

■ **Check plants for signs of pests and diseases.** Routine garden inspections make it wonderfully easy to nip problems in the bud. Tour your garden every few days at least, looking closely at plants for insect damage or signs of disease. Look closely at leaves for signs of infestations, making sure to turn

them over to check the undersides. Identify problems (bring samples to your local garden center or Cooperative Extension Service office if you're not sure what you've discovered) and take steps to correct them before they get out of hand. Powdery mildew and other fungal diseases can be particularly troubling in late summer. Deal with them by picking off and discarding diseased leaves, and/or applying an organic fungicide like sulfur.

■ **Evaluate your garden with an eye for improvements.** The garden is now full of life. Perennials have filled out. Annuals are big and bushy. Containers overflow with flowers. If your garden doesn't look good now, it never will. Take time to analyze what you see and decide what you like and don't like. To start, ask yourself these questions: Do your plantings create a sense of enclosure and privacy, and are those qualities you value? Does your color scheme work within each bed and among the different areas of the garden? How does your garden look from inside the house, and can you improve views of it from indoors by adding or rearranging plants? Write your answers in a garden diary or notebook, or take photos to refer to later. Records of what's in bloom and how the garden looks will be invaluable when you begin making decisions about improvements.

■ **Study bulb catalogues and order garlic and flowering bulbs and corms to plant this fall.** Bulb catalogues seem to arrive earlier every year, but if you haven't ordered yet, now is the time to get busy so you'll have bulbs on hand for fall planting.

Perennials and annuals at the height of summer.

*Garden*Magic

SAVING SEEDS FOR NEXT YEAR'S GARDEN

Collecting and saving seeds for next year's garden—or to share with friends—is a pleasant activity that can also save you money. Seeds of many different plants are ready to harvest in late summer and autumn. Keep in mind that not all the seeds you collect will produce seedlings that look exactly like their parents—but that

Spider flower (*Cleome hasslerana* 'Violet Queen').

can be part of the fun. Seed from species plants almost always "comes true," meaning it yields seedlings that resemble the parent plant. Seeds collected from cultivars may or may not come true; open-pollinated cultivars, sometimes listed in catalogues as "OP," do come true, provided they're planted far enough away from other plants in the same species. If they're planted too close, insects may carry pollen between the two plants, and you may be surprised when you grow out the seedlings. Seeds collected from hybrids typically do not come true.

There are several methods of seed collection. Clip browning seedheads of plants such as lovage or dill and place them in a small brown paper bag. Label the bag with the plant's name, fold over the top, close it with a paper clip, and place the bag in a warm dry place. When the seeds ripen, they will fall into the bag. Although some seeds are ready in a couple of days, most seed collected nearly ripe will take 2 to 3 weeks to dry. Shake the seedheads in the bag to loosen any seeds that have not dropped. Then discard the seedheads and store the seed in the bag or in a clean envelope, labeled with the name of the parent and the collection date.

Plants like spider flower (*Cleome hasslerana*) and love-in-a-mist (*Nigella damascena*) bear seeds in capsules that are ready to harvest when the capsules turn brown and begin to split. Don't wait too long to harvest them, however, since once the capsules split, ripe seed can tumble to the ground. (These plants self-sow, so in a good site you'll have another chance to collect next year.) Drying the capsules in a brown paper bag in a warm, dry room is the easiest method. Collect the capsules when they are browning and beginning to split. When they are completely dry and open, tap the seeds into a bag and throw away the capsule. Label the bags or seed envelopes and keep them in a cool, dry cupboard or drawer.

Crush fleshy fruits that contain seeds—including holly berries, barberries, and rose hips—with your fingers, then remove the seeds from the flesh, and wash them in warm water. After drying place them in a plastic bag with some dry sand. Then refrigerate the seeds until you're ready to sow them.

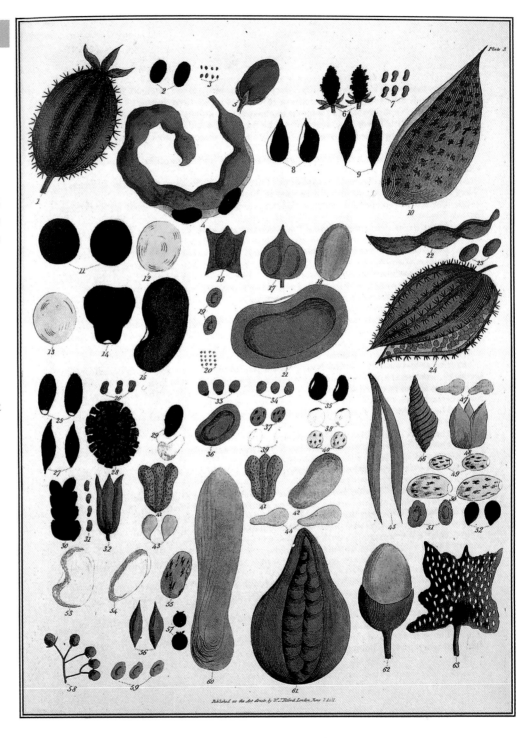

Published as the Act directs by W.Tilford London June 7 1811.

TREES AND SHRUBS

■ **Train wayward vines.** While some vines stick closely to their trellis or other support, others send their stems far and wide. To redirect a wayward perennial or annual vine, first note whether it naturally grows in a clockwise or counterclockwise direction, then train the stems accordingly. For example, honeysuckles (*Lonicera* spp.) and Japanese wisteria (*Wisteria floribunda*) twine clockwise, whereas Chinese wisteria (*W. sinensis*), bittersweet (*Celastrus* spp.), and five-leaf akebia (*Akebia quinata*) grow counterclockwise. Secure stems and branches to the support, being careful not to damage the plant.

■ **Stop pruning shrubs and trees.** Pruning stimulates new growth, so stop cutting back trees and shrubs 6 weeks before the first fall frost to give new growth time to harden. New growth too late in the season will be susceptible to frost damage.

■ **Don't fertilize shrubs and trees after mid-month.** Like late-season pruning, fertilizing late in the season also stimulates tender new growth, which can be damaged by frost in fall. It's best to stop fertilizing at least 6 weeks

Honeysuckle *Lonicera* × *heckrottii*.

before the first frost to get plants ready for their winter's rest.

■ **Consider adding shrubs to flower borders.** While plantings of perennials and annuals are in full bloom, it is a good time to decide whether larger-scale plants would add appeal. Shrubs add spring or summer flowers as well as winter character to beds and borders. Consider adding larger shrubs to provide plants with a handsome backdrop for flowers or smaller ones in mid-border or as edgings. Roses, viburnums, hydrangeas, potentillas, and small lilacs—especially dainty, disease-resistant *Syringa pubescens* ssp. *patula* 'Miss Kim'—are all good choices for sunny gardens. Try purple-leaved smoke tree (*Cotinus coggygria* 'Royal Purple' or 'Velvet Cloak') for a spot of purple foliage; for the best foliage show, cut smoke trees to the ground in late winter. Bluebeard (*Caryopteris* × *clandonensis*) is another excellent choice for sun. For shade, rhododendrons and azaleas are obvious choices, but don't overlook summersweet (*Clethra alnifolia*), mountain laurel (*Kalmia latifolia*), and oakleaf hydrangea (*Hydrangea quercifolia*).

Oxyacantha rosea superba. | Ribes Sanguineum.

Rhododendron Ponticum. | Stephora Tetraptera.

■ **Divide or transplant Oriental poppies.** These plants, which disappear after blooming in early summer, produce new foliage in late summer, indicating that it's time to divide overgrown clumps.

■ **Add extra fall-blooming perennials to the garden.** Potted chrysanthemums, also called fall, or garden mums, are widely available and can be popped in anywhere to add a spot of dramatic fall color. These perennials are commonly grown as annuals, because many of the cultivars sold aren't hardy. Fall-planted mums won't be well-enough established to survive the winter; if you want mums that will behave like perennials, ask for them at a reputable nursery, and plant them early. Garden centers also offer pots of blooming asters, sedums—including 'Autumn Joy' and *S. spectabile* 'Brilliant'—and other fall-blooming perennials that are

Many gardeners plant shallow-rooted annuals over Oriental poppies to fill the spots left when their foliage goes dormant. If your poppies need dividing, try to site annuals around the clumps so you can divide with minimal disturbance.

great for extending the bloom season into fall. These flowers enrich the garden palette with deep red, purple, orange, and gold, and harmonize with both evergreens and colorful deciduous shrubs like fothergilla and oakleaf hydrangea. Late summer is also a good time to look around for perennials that bloom in other seasons: you're likely to find good deals on plants that nursery owners would like to sell before the end of the growing season. Try to get new perennials planted at least 6 weeks before the first fall frost to give them time to become established. After the ground freezes, mulch them over winter with evergreen boughs or weed-free straw.

■ **Sow self-sowing annuals where you'd like them to appear next spring and summer.** Now is a good time to sow many cool-weather annuals, especially those that will self-sow in subsequent years. Either start with packets of new seeds or, if you have these

Not all flowering tobaccos are fragrant, but *Nicotiana* × *sanderae* 'Fragrant Cloud' was selected for this characteristic.

plants in the garden already but would like to have them in another spot, pick ripe seedpods. Before sowing, loosen patches of soil and rake them smooth; then sprinkle on the seeds. Forget-me-nots (*Myosotis sylvatica*) look good near daffodils and tulips; flowering tobaccos (*Nicotiana* spp.) are lovely near paths and patios where you can inhale their evening perfume; love-in-a-mist (*Nigella damascena*) weaves through perennial borders with delicacy and finesse; spider flower (*Cleome hasslerana*) stands tall at the back of the border.

■ **Cut flowers to bring indoors.** With sharp pruners or scissors, cut flower stems in the morning after the dew has dried, but while they are still turgid; avoid harvesting after the temperature has risen above 80°F. Carry a bucket of water with you so you can put cut stems into water immediately. To prolong vase life, place cut flowers in a deep container filled with tepid water, ideally immersing them right up to the flowers, then set them aside for 6 to 8 hours before arranging. When ready to display flowers, remove all leaves

*Garden*Magic

ATTRACT BUTTERFLIES WITH NECTAR FLOWERS

When studying your garden at its August peak you may notice visual holes in your design. It can be hard to decide what to plant in those bare spots: why not add some colorful nectar flowers that will help draw butterflies? The perennials listed below usually flower in late summer or fall, although a few bloom earlier.

When you're choosing your plants, consider that while butterflies do drink the nectar of non-native purple loosestrife (*Lythrum salicaria*), this is not a good enough reason to grow it. This vigorous plant self-seeds to such an extent that it has endangered many North American wetlands. For years, gardeners purchased sterile cultivars, believing that they would not reproduce. Research now shows that while sterile plants can't be pollinated by other sterile plants, they can produce seeds if pollinated by the ubiquitous species and vice versa. Many states have banned the sale of purple loosestrife: Follow their example by keeping it off your property.

Tall Perennials

The flowers listed below grow to over 3 feet tall. Use them for the back or the middle of borders, toward the center of island beds, and in wild gardens.

Asters (*Aster* spp.) provide nectar and food for butterfly larvae, plus their masses of showy yellow-centered lavender, purple, and pink flowers add loads of late-summer to fall color. New England aster (*A. novae-angliae*) ranges from 4 to 6 feet; New York aster (*A. novi-belgii*) is 3 to 5 feet tall. Both may need staking.

False sunflower or Oxeye (*Heliopsis helianthoides*) is a 4-foot-tall yellow-flowered perennial that blooms from midsummer to fall.

Goldenrods (*Solidago* spp.) are native wildflowers that range from 2 to 6 feet tall. Their trusses of tiny golden flowers, borne in summer and fall, attract both butterflies and beneficial insects.

Butterflies love easy-to-grow purple coneflower (*Echinacea purpurea*).

Joe-Pye weeds (*Eupatorim* spp.) are moisture-loving native wildflowers that stand 5 to 6 feet high in full sun, taller in part shade. *E. maculatum* 'Gateway' is an attractive cultivar with huge purple flower heads and red stems.

Orange coneflower (*Rudbeckia nitida* 'Herbstsonne') attracts masses of butterflies—especially monarchs—to its 3- to 4-inch yellow flowerheads, borne atop 7-foot stems from midsummer to fall.

Perennial phlox (*Phlox* spp.) bloom from summer to early fall in shades of white, pink, red, blue, and purple. Mildew-resistant cultivars of garden phlox (*P. paniculata*), such as 'David', or meadow phlox (*P. maculata*), are mostly free of this fungal disease (it causes powdery, then yellowed spots, followed by defoliation).

Sneezeweed (*Helenium autumnale*) produces daisylike yellow, orange, or red-brown flowers on 3- to 6-foot plants.

Medium to Short Perennials

The following are ideal for the middle to front of a border, as well as for the wild garden. Common wildflowers, including Queen Ann's lace (*Daucus carota*), ox-eye daisies (*Leucanthemum vulgare*), and clovers (*Trifolium* spp.) also provide food for larvae or nectar for adult butterflies.

Butterfly weed (*Asclepias tuberosa*) is an 18- to 36-inch-tall native perennial with bright orange flowers. Monarch butterflies visit the flowers and their larvae feed on the foliage.

Catmint (*Nepeta* × *faassenii*) bears airy clusters of lavender-blue flowers in early to midsummer. Plants rebloom in late summer and fall if they are cut to within several inches of the ground after the first flush of flowers.

Gayfeathers (*Liatris* spp.) are 1- to 3-foot native wildflowers with dense, narrow spikes of rosy purple or white flowers.

Mints (*Mentha* spp.) are perennials approximately 2 feet tall, with aromatic leaves and pale purple flowers that attract both butterflies and beneficial insects. Beware: Grow mints in containers sunk in the soil, with at least an inch or two of the edge jutting above it, or these fast-spreading plants will take over your whole garden bed.

Orange coneflowers (*Rudbeckia* spp.) are all good butterfly plants. Two species are commonly called black-eyed Susans: *R. hirta*, generally grown as an annual, has yellow, orange, bronze, brown, and bicolored cultivars. *R. fulgida*, a drought-tolerant perennial, has yellow "petals," or rays, and blackish disk flowers.

Purple coneflower (*Echinacea purpurea*) is a drought-resistant 2- to 4-foot native wildflower with daisylike flowers with brownish centers, or cones, and purple-pink or white petals.

Showy stonecrop (*Sedum spectabile*) is a versatile 2- to 3-foot-tall perennial with multi-season interest. Butterflies adore its 3- to 6-inch heads of pink, red, or white flowers . They also enjoy *S.* 'Autumn Joy', with its salmon-turning-to-burgundy flowers, and *S.* 'Ruby Glow', with its purplish-gray leaves and deep red fall flowers.

Tickseeds (*Coreopsis* spp.) bear daisylike flowers in yellows to golds on 2- to 3-foot plants. Deadhead plants to encourage rebloom from summer to fall.

Yarrows (*Achillea* spp.) are tough drought-tolerant perennials with flat-topped clusters of white, yellow, gold, pink, or maroon flowers that butterflies can easily land on. Plants stand 1 to 4 or more feet tall, and spread fast in full sun and well-drained soil.

that will be below the waterline of the vase. Recutting stems under water also prolongs vase life, because it prevents air bubbles from blocking the flow of water up the stems: As you hold each stem under water, cut 1 to 2 inches off the end. Then arrange the flowers in a container filled with water that has been treated with a commercial floral preservative, to lengthen vase life.

If you don't have preservative, add ¼ teaspoon of bleach and 1 tablespoon of granulated sugar per gallon of water.

■ **Plant crown imperial** (*Fritillaria imperialis*). This spring-flowering bulb becomes available for purchase in late summer, and is best planted soon after shipment so the fleshy, scaly bulbs won't dry out and new roots can grow. Handle the fragile bulbs carefully, planting them about 8 inches deep in full sun to partial shade. Excellent soil drainage is a must. If you've had problems with rot in past years, try planting the bulbs on their sides so that water doesn't collect in the center of the bulb around the scales.

■ **Plant fall crocuses and colchicums as soon as bulbs are available.** Meadow saffron (*Colchicum autumnale*) bears white or lavender flowers in September and is shade-tolerant, deer-proof, and hardy in Zones 4 to 9. Fall crocuses, including *Crocus speciosus, C. byzantinus*, and *C. kotschyanus,* also tolerate partial or deciduous shade, and flower in October. Saffron crocus (*C. sativus*), hardy to Zone 6, blooms in October and has a 3-branched stigma that is dried to make saffron. Plant fall crocuses 4 inches deep, preferably among low ground covers.

Corona Imperialis
Polyanthos.

G a r d e n   A l m a n a c

FRUITS AND VEGETABLES

■ **Direct-seed turnips for a fall harvest.** Sow seeds ¼ inch deep and 1 inch apart, then thin plants to 4 inches apart once seedlings appear. Try 'Hakurei' raw for its sweetness and crisp texture. It matures in just 38 days, making it suitable for cold-climate gardens. For repeated harvests sow seeds every 2 weeks until a month before the last frost date.

'Purple Top White Globe', an heirloom turnip cultivar.

■ **Continue harvesting herbs.** Ideally, herbs should be harvested before they bloom, when their flavor is most intense, but harvest them—flowers and all—if they get ahead of you. (Basil, thyme, rosemary, oregano, and most other culinary herbs bear edible flowers, which can be added to cooked dishes as well as to salads.) Try to harvest in the morning, after the dew has dried but before the sun is at its hottest.

- **Harvest green lima beans.** The end of the pod opposite the stem should feel spongy when pressed between your thumb and forefinger. The pod should bulge a bit and measure ⅛ inch to ¼ inch thick. For fresh beans, don't wait until the pod yellows.

- **Harvest cucumbers, eggplants, and peppers as they ripen, so new ones can develop.** Cut fruits from the plants—don't pull them off—as pulling on the plants will damage the roots.

While purple-black is the typical color for eggplants, cultivars with white, pale green, and lavender fruits are available.

- **Propagate strawberries or weed them and thin out the runners.** Every 3 years, it's a good idea to rotate your strawberry patch to a new spot; this reduces problems with pests and diseases. You don't need to buy new plants each time they move to new ground, though. Dig up healthy-looking runners that have rooted near the mother plants, taking care not to harm the roots. Detach these runners from the mother with pruners or a sharp knife and replant them 18 inches apart (12 inches for alpines) in fresh, rich, well-drained soil amended with compost or well-rotted manure. Discard the old plants. If you're not rotating your strawberry plants, cut off the runners and keep the patch weed-free to lessen the competition for soil nutrients. Strawberry patches get overcrowded, weedy, and unproductive fast, so it's important to keep up with these basic tasks. Avoid planting more strawberries than you can care for.

- **Prune away berry canes that have finished fruiting.** Raspberry and blackberry canes fruit only once, then die. To make room for new canes, cut those that have already fruited to the ground.

Garden Almanac

*Garden*Bounty

PRESERVING BASIL IN ICE AND OIL

Gardeners who try to dry basil are often disappointed at the results, because basil tends to lose color and flavor in the drying process. Fortunately, you can savor basil's pungent flavor and fragrance all winter long if you take time to prepare trays of basil ice cubes from now until the first fall frost. Harvest the basil and sort through the leaves, rejecting any with signs of insect damage or disease, as well as those with holes, spots, and discoloration; wash thoroughly. To make the cubes, blend equal parts basil leaves and water in a blender. Freeze the mixture in an ice-cube tray, then pop the cubes out of the ice tray and into a labeled, zippered plastic bag; store in the freezer. When you need basil for soup, stew, or tomato sauce, drop a couple of cubes into the simmering mixture.

Another way to preserve basil is in oil. Make a paste by pureeing two cups of fresh basil

leaves and 1 cup of olive oil in a food processor or a blender. Place the paste in ice-cube trays or spoon it out on a cookie sheet for freezing, then transfer the frozen morsels to a labeled container and use as needed for sauces and other recipes. Or simply store it all in a freezer-safe container: In this case, to soften the paste for spooning, microwave the container for about 15 seconds on High. You can also freeze a traditional pesto, which is made by adding 2 cloves of chopped garlic, 3 or 4 tablespoons of pine nuts, and 1 teaspoon of salt to the basil mixture before pureeing. Prior to serving the pesto, stir in ½ cup of freshly grated Parmesan cheese. Experiment with these measurements to create a pesto that suits your family's taste. I often leave out the cheese and use walnuts when there are no pine nuts in the cupboard.

Digging In

Compost, the gardener's gold, is an effective soil amendment that fertilizes, conditions, and improves soil structure. Incorporating compost into heavy clay soil promotes better drainage, while adding it to sandy soil aids water retention.

Rich, dark, soil-like compost begins as a mix of yard and kitchen waste. Grass clippings, leaves, spent annuals, healthy perennial and shrub prunings, and even weeds are suitable for composting. (Avoid adding diseased plant materials or weeds that are going to seed.) Kitchen materials that can go to your compost pile include fruit and vegetable scraps, eggshells, and coffee grounds. (Don't add meat, fat, or pet droppings to your pile, as they will attract vermin.) Once they are completely decomposed, these unpromising materials turn into nutrient-rich humus that will lead to a healthier, flourishing garden.

The process of decomposition depends on a host of bacteria, fungi, and other microscopic organisms—or "microherd." Bigger creatures that work the heap include earthworms, slugs, spiders, ants, flies, and other organisms. The process works best when several conditions are present.

A conventional compost pile should measure at least 3 feet on all sides so that it will generate enough heat to decompose the contents quickly. Decomposing matter should be slightly damp but not soggy, and have adequate oxygen, which the microherd requires to do its work. In dry or windy weather you may need to water the pile periodically to maintain moisture levels. Aerate, by turning the pile once or twice a month, to speed decomposition and raise the internal temperature of the compost; at 150° to 160°F, the compost's internal combustion should destroy any weed seeds or disease organisms inadvertently included with the plant material. It's okay to just pile up materials and leave them for up to a year; the microherd will take care of the rest, but this no-turn method, also called cold composting, won't kill weed seeds.

Another means of hastening decomposition is to shred the waste before putting it in the pile to increase the surface area available for microbial activity. The ratio of carbon to nitrogen, another crucial factor, influences the breakdown of waste. If you're composting sawdust, straw, or even unshredded tree leaves, consider adding nitrogen to the pile to encourage decomposition. Cow manure, blood meal, and fresh grass clippings are high in nitrogen, so adding them to the compost pile speeds

PEST DEFENSE

disintegration. Finished compost has an alkaline pH of about 7.1 to 7.5, so it's usually unnecessary to sweeten the compost pile with lime.

Most gardeners prefer to keep their compost contained. Many options exist, ranging from expensive rotating barrels to chicken-wire holding areas and plastic garbage bags. In addition to ventilation holes, the best composting devices include a lid to keep out excessive moisture and provide easy access to the finished compost.

Use compost as a soil-enriching mulch on flower beds and borders, or as a soil amendment in the vegetable garden; dig it into the soil when you are creating a new garden. Or turn it into fertilizer by placing a shovelful of compost in a burlap bag and then setting it in a bucket of water. Let it "steep" until the water is tan or light brown. Return the used compost to a new pile, and use the liquid fertilizer to water container plants or houseplants.

In gardening, as in sports, the best defense is a good offense. Plants that are in topnotch form and growing vigorously are better able to resist attack by pests and diseases. Mulching, regular watering, and feeding are all excellent ways to keep plants healthy and vigorous. Handling plants carefully is another valuable, yet all-too-often neglected, line of defense. Avoid tearing, crushing, bruising, or otherwise damaging leaves, stems, flowers, and fruit. Disease-causing organisms such as fungi can easily infect plants through torn leaves and bruised stems. Don't work among plants when they are wet, either, or you risk spreading disease-causing fungal spores from plant to plant on the water that clings to your clothes and tools. It's also good practice to clean tools routinely to avoid spreading diseases.

Encouraging populations of beneficial insects such as parasitic wasps, lady beetles, and lacewings—along with spiders—is a great way to control insect pests. Plants that are rich in nectar and pollen, such as mints, dill, and yarrow, attract adult beneficials. Routinely inspect plants—every other day or so during the height of the season—to catch problems before they get out of hand. A blast of water from the hose may be all it takes to control mites and aphids. Handpicking works for larger pests; drop the culprits into a jar of soapy water. For more serious infestations, try soap spray or one of the biological insecticides available at garden centers.

SEPTEMBER'S TASKS

THE WHOLE GARDEN
- Continue watering your garden as needed during dry weather.
- Continue collecting seeds for next year's garden.
- Continue checking regularly for signs of pests and diseases.
- Continue weeding your beds.
- Cover water gardens with netting.

TREES AND SHRUBS
- Plant roses as well as other shrubs and trees.
- Cut roses with fall bloom to bring indoors.
- Water newly planted trees and shrubs once a week.
- Water established trees and shrubs only in periods of drought.

FLOWERS AND GRASSES
- Mow the lawn frequently and feed it to keep it in topnotch form.
- De-thatch and aerate your lawn.
- Sow grass seed.
- Cut back ragged-looking perennials.
- Divide perennials.
- Divide peonies.
- Uproot spent annuals and toss them on the compost pile.
- Sow annuals for bloom next year.
- Dig tender bulbs when the leaves die back.
- Plant tulips.
- Move indoors any houseplants that summered outdoors.

FRUITS AND VEGETABLES
- Continue direct-seeding lettuce, endive, escarole, and spinach.
- Harvest the last of your basil before frost.
- Harvest fall raspberries (*Rubus* spp.).
- Before a hard frost, harvest fava bean plants.
- Begin harvesting cold-tolerant vegetables such as kale and Brussels sprouts.
- Harvest pumpkins and winter squash.
- Dig up and pot rosemary to overwinter indoors.
- Clean up areas of the vegetable garden that have finished producing.

Septe

September bouquets are among the loveliest and liveliest of the year. Their fullness marks summer's end and the bounty of the harvest. This month's Furber print displays many plants that thrive in North America. Annual African marigolds (*Tagetes erecta*)—actually native to Mexico and Central America—quickly grow into bushy, 2-foot-tall mounds of deeply cut, scented foliage and big double yellow or orange flower heads. Furber combines Johnny-jump-ups, which he calls heartsease, and autumn crocuses, or meadow saffron (*Colchicum* spp.) in yellow, checkered, white, and double forms. While *Colchicum byzantinum* is only hardy to Zone 6, *C. autumnale* and *C. speciosum* are hardy in Zones 4 to 9, making them suitable for planting in most regions of the United States. *C. speciosum* 'Album' is a particularly choice form of meadow saffron, with large cup-shaped white flowers, yellow stamens, and green flower tubes. Roses, hollyhocks, soapwort, gentians, cardinal flower, passionflowers, amaranthus, and mulleins also bring old-fashioned charm to Furber's bouquet, as well as to garden beds and borders.

Lavish cut-flower arrangements are not the only natural phenomenon to result from cooling outdoor temperatures. Consider those swarms of multicolored Asian lady beetles making themselves at home near windows and doors on the south and west sides of the house. Looking for a cozy place to spend the winter they crowd the swags above windows, although their native habitat is the base of trees and sides of cliffs. These little insects—handsome in shades of orange and red, with or without dark spots—kill scales, aphids, and mealybugs. If you step on them, however, they discharge a yellow blood that can stain your carpets. The United States Department of Agriculture released the first wave of Asian lady beetles in the South in the 1970s, but generations of the insects gradually spread north. As long as lady beetles lend their beneficial presence to my garden, they're welcome to winter in the folds of my curtains.

1. Red Sow Bread.
2. White Sow Bread.
3. White Corn-marigold.
4. Ever Tree Primrose.
5. Sour leav'd Geranium.
6. Quill'd African Marigold.
7. Hearts ease.
8. Shrub Cotton.
9. Shefford's Hester Auricula.
10. Virginian Birthwort.
11. Virginian upright Bramble.
12. Scarlet Indian Cane.
13. White Colchicum.
14. Bean Caper.
15. All red Amaranthus.
16. Double white Soapwort.
17. Yellow Indian Cane.
18. Virginian Poke.
19. Gentianella.
20. White monthly Rose.
21. Yellow Amaranthus.
22. Oriental Arsmart.
23. Broad leav'd Cardinal.
24. Yellow Colchicum.
25. Hardy golden-Rod.
26. White Althæa frutex.
27. Chequer'd Colchicum.
28. Yellow Colutea.
29. Dwarf Pomgranate.
30. Strip'd single Female balsom.
31. African Marigold.
32. Humour's glory Auricula.
33. White flower Moth Mullein.
34. Double Colchicum.
35. Three leav'd Passion Flower.

SEPTEMBER

Design'd by Pet. Casteels.

From the Collection of Rob.t Furber Gardner at Kensington. 1730.

Engrav'd by H. Fletcher.

Spotted toad lilies (*Tricyrtis* spp.) open and plumey flowers of ornamental grasses such as *Miscanthus* sway above leaves rustling in the wind. Roses rebloom, while our bluegrass lawn grows so fast we mow it 3 times a week. Sweet golden fall raspberries, originally intended for the dinner table, instead go from hand to mouth as quickly as they're picked. September's spurt of gardening activity follows the August lull; important chores like planting shrubs, repairing the lawn, and preparing houseplants for indoor living fill stolen weekday moments and cram weekend hours. Autumn dwells in cool nights and earthy smells.

THE WHOLE GARDEN

■ **Continue weeding your beds.** Keep an eye out for so-called winter weeds, including dead nettles and chickweed, which germinate in fall once temperatures cool. They grow slowly over winter and then bloom and set seed fairly early in spring, often before you've started spring weeding. Pulling up the seedlings now will prevent the growth of yet another generation of weeds next season.

■ **Cover water gardens with netting.** Spread plastic netting over ornamental ponds to catch any leaves that might otherwise fall into the water. As leaves decompose in the water they produce gases that can stress or kill your fish, especially if gasses are trapped under a layer of ice.

TIP: PONDS While natural ponds don't need a routine cleanup, artificial water gardens do, and fall is an ideal time to tackle this task. Water gardens with more than an inch of debris at the bottom are especially in need of cleaning out. If yours is well balanced, meaning it contains plenty of plants and not too many fish, it will only need cleaning out every few years. If you have lots of fish, plan on tackling this task at least every other year.

S e p t e m b e r

TREES AND SHRUBS

- **Plant roses as well as other shrubs and trees.** While spring is the traditional season for planting, fall is also an excellent time to add roses and other woody plants to the garden. For best results with roses, select a site that receives early-morning sun; it dries the dew on the leaves early in the day, thus hindering the development of powdery mildew and black spot. A damp, shady location provides conditions where these fungal diseases—the bane of many rose enthusiasts—flourish.

- **Cut roses with fall bloom to bring indoors.** Double your pleasure by enjoying the last, lovely blooms of the season indoors as well as out.

Magnolia denudata, Malus sylvestris, and *Chaenomeles japonica.*

■ **Water newly planted trees and shrubs once a week.** Remember that tree and shrub roots keep growing after the top of the plant has gone dormant—they grow until the soil temperature drops to about 50°F—and regular watering is essential to establishing these plants. A thorough soaking once a week is more valuable to newly planted trees and shrubs than lightly watering every day because it encourages the growth of deep, far-reaching roots and thus better-established, drought-tolerant plants. Never water trees and shrubs by spraying them with a hand-held hose, since this tends to encourage shallow-rooted plants that will suffer in dry weather. Instead lay your garden hose at the base of the plant, turn the water pressure to a trickle, and water the plant until the roots are thoroughly soaked. The amount of time to spend watering each plant varies according to the type of soil and the size of the root mass. After an hour, check to see if the water has reached the roots by carefully removing some soil around the plant's drip line with a trowel. If in doubt, water more.

■ **Water established trees and shrubs only in periods of drought.** If June, July, and August were months with little rain, and September is also dry, then go ahead and water established plants thoroughly, trickling the water around each plant as you would for a newly planted specimen. If you irrigate your property with a sprinkler system, stop watering by the end of the month. Fall rains plus frequent irrigation may put too much moisture into the tree bark, causing it to split during winter freeze-and-thaw cycles.

TIP: Oaks (*Quercus* spp.) are ideal choices for wildlife-friendly gardens. Not only do squirrels, chipmunks, and other mammals relish the acorns, a surprising variety of birds eat them, too. Many birds eat the insects attracted to oak trees. In spring, look for rose-breasted grosbeaks eating the male flowers. Oaks also provide nesting sites for birds as well as for mammals such as flying squirrels. Hollies (*Ilex* spp.) and other berry-bearing trees and shrubs also feed birds and other wildlife.

*Garden*Magic

TREE PEONIES

September, the month for planting and dividing herbaceous peonies, is also the time to plant tree peonies. Unlike herbaceous peonies, which die to the ground each winter, tree peonies (*Paeonia suffruticosa*) are woody plants—although they are not, as their common name suggests, trees. Native to China, tree peonies are 3- to 7-foot-tall shrubs that can spread to 3 or 4 feet in width. They bear lavish, 5- to 10-inch-diameter flowers between mid-May and early June, about 2 weeks before herbaceous types bloom. The flowers are set off against somewhat coarse yet handsome compound leaves; these are from 12 to 18 inches long, with deeply cut lobes. The foliage remains attractive all season and is usually grayish green, although it ranges from dull to glossy and yellowish- to purple-tinted green.

Tree peony 'Hino Tsukasa'.

Tree peony flowers have a satiny, crepe-paper-like texture and can be single, semi-double, or double; many double flowers are so large and heavy that the individual flowers must be staked. The blossoms, which may or may not be fragrant, come in a mind-boggling variety of colors, including pink, red, magenta, lavender, purple, blackish purple, yellow, and green. Many blooms feature delicate color gradations, and single and semi-double forms usually have a large, showy boss, or cluster, of long golden stamens in the center. Flower shape, size, and strength of fragrance can vary on a single plant as well as from year to year.

For the best selection of cultivars, plan on ordering by mail. Tree peonies are expensive, but the plants are long-lived, and good-quality cultivars are well worth the price. Choosing which ones to grow can be a challenge. The following 3 cultivars will give you a taste of the wonders that await you: Rare and distinctive, 'Pea Green' opens aqua-green but turns to olive-flecked purple at the base when fully opened. The fragrant double flowers, which fade to white after a few days, are 5 to 6 inches wide, borne on a 4- to 5-foot-tall plant. For size, consider 'Wine-Warmed Radiant Beauty'. It has purple-pink, anemone-like blooms of up to 10 inches across on a vigorous, freely blooming plant 7 feet tall. The petals vary in size and are reddish purple at the base. Yellow tree peonies may be cultivars of *Paeonia lutea*. Lotus-shaped 'Champion of Yellow Flowers' has pale yellow petals with a purplish tint and purple flecks at the base. Blossoms measure 6 inches across on 5-foot-tall plants.

Best planted in September and October, tree peonies are hardy in Zones 3 to 9. To plant them, first scout a location where they can thrive undisturbed, since they don't transplant well. In the right site, tree peonies can live more than 100 years. Choose a location in partial shade to shield the flowers from the hot afternoon sun, but make sure that from Zone 5 north plants receive 4 to 5 hours of direct sunlight daily. Tree peonies need rich, loamy soil that is high in organic matter. A slightly alkaline pH—7.0 to 7.5—is best. Moist, well-drained soil is essential because without proper drainage root rot will kill the plants. Select a site away from trees so the tree peonies don't have to compete for soil nutrients.

To plant, dig a hole roughly 24 inches deep and wide. Make a mound in the base of the hole tall enough for the plant's roots to spread out. Place the plant on the mound with the roots outstretched, making sure that the graft union, which looks like a swelling at the base of the plant, is at least 4 to 5 inches below ground. (Tree peony cultivars are usually grafted onto the rootstock of herbaceous peonies.) By planting deeply, you are making it possible for the grafted stock to take root and discouraging the rootstock from sprouting. Fill the hole, patting the soil gently but firmly around the plant's roots and watering it in. Leave 4 to 5 feet between plants so they have room to grow; they may not reach their full height for 10 to 20 years.

Water your tree peony during dry weather for its first growing season. (Plants may not bloom the first or even the second season.) Tree peonies have roots 3 to 5 feet deep and can seek water on their own, so once they're established it's not necessary to water them. Fertilize with compost or well-rotted manure. Plants in Zone 5 and colder need winter protection: Stake the main stems and then surround the plant with a chicken wire cage. Fill the cage with straw, pine needles, or oak leaves.

■ **Mow the lawn frequently and feed it to keep it in topnotch form.** Cool weather means most lawn grasses are in a period of fast growth, so plan to mow at least once a week. Keep the mower set to 3 inches for most grasses and use the mulching attachment to avoid the need to bag and dispose of the clippings. A mulching mower, or a mulching attachment for your existing mower, also buys you free food for your lawn, as the fine pieces of grass it spreads on the lawn break down into a high-nitrogen fertilizer. The key to fertilizing your lawn effectively with grass clippings is frequent mowing; it keeps the cuttings small so that they decompose quickly and easily and do not build up into thatch. A fall dose of balanced fertilizer (5-5-5) is also in order. Slow-release chemical lawn fertilizers are available at nurseries and garden centers. They also carry organic options, including aged, processed manure, fish meal, or commercial sifted compost. If you opt for compost, make sure it is weed-free. I twice bought organic compost that had not reached high enough temperatures to kill the weed seeds. I paid for that mistake with hours and hours of extra weeding.

■ **De-thatch and aerate your lawn.** Thatch isn't a problem in well-managed lawns with healthy soil, but improper lawn care—cutting the lawn too short, overwatering, and especially overfertilizing—can cause it to develop. Thatch is a crust of old, partially decomposed grass stems and leaves that becomes a hotbed for weeds, pests, and diseases. You can buy a de-thatching attachment for your lawn mower, remove thatch by hand with a thatch rake, or rent a power rake. After de-thatching, aerate your lawn to improve the soil and help the grass stay healthy. (Your lawn becomes compacted through regular mowings and just by your walking on it.) When you aerate, you remove plugs of dirt, allowing air into the soil and making space for the grass roots to grow. For best results, rent a power plugger. Step-on core cultivators aren't efficient enough to make them practical for a large area. If your lawn is irrigated, mark the sprinkler heads before aerating to save on costly repairs to the system. Leave the soil plugs you've removed on the lawn—they'll break down quickly—

and spread a thin layer of topsoil, sand, or compost over the lawn to improve the soil. It, too, will work its way down and disappear.

- **Sow grass seed.** If you prepared soil for a new lawn in July, now is the time to sow. For the most vigorous types for your area—or the latest disease- or pest-resistant selections—consult a county agent at your local Cooperative Extension Service.

- **Cut back ragged-looking perennials.** When touring your garden you may notice that slugs have feasted on your hostas and powdery mildew has turned the fresh green leaves of your false sunflowers

Hostas thrive for years without needing to be divided, but if you cut slug-eaten specimens to the ground, early fall is a good time to divide them.

(*Heliopsis* spp.) dirty white. The growing season is not yet over, but it's time for nasty-looking plants to retire for the year. Cut back slug-damaged leaves on hostas. If the entire plant looks ugly, cut it to the ground. Cut down fall mums that have finished blooming, too. Likewise, cut down the false sunflowers, the mildewed phlox, and any other diseased plants. You may have to sacrifice a few blooms, but tidying up a bit will improve the appearance of your garden

overall. To save time when cutting down swathes of tough, tall perennials like false sunflowers—vigorous plants that spread by underground stems or rhizomes—use a gas-powered blade trimmer to do the job.

- **Divide perennials.** Daylilies, phlox, and Oriental poppies (*Papaver orientale*) can all be divided now. Depending on the size of the plant, use two garden forks, a spade, or a knife with a long, sharp blade to split the plant into divisions.

GardenMagic

FORCING PAPERWHITES FOR HOLIDAY BLOOMS

If you'd like to have fragrant, fresh flowers blooming on a windowsill at Halloween, Thanksgiving, and Christmas, begin forcing paperwhite narcissus, a daffodil with small clustered blooms on top of long green stems. Paperwhites are easy to force indoors. Buy a shallow bulb bowl without drainage holes and fill it ⅔ full with gravel, pebbles, glass marbles, or fancy polished stones. Set bulbs on top with the pointed side up, fitting in as many as you comfortably can. Fill in around the bulbs with the stones but leave the tops exposed. Add water up to the base of the bulbs and keep it at that level. Put the bowl in a cool spot until green shoots are visible, then move it to a sunny place like a windowsill. In about 3 more weeks, you'll have lovely, sweetly fragrant white flowers. You might also plant 'Soleil d'Or' for fragrant yellow flowers. Repeat the process every couple of weeks for a continuous display through the fall and winter.

You can also force paperwhites individually in forcing vases, which are available through mail-order catalogues and at garden shops and home-furnishing chain stores. (There are forcing vases for many different bulbs, including crocuses, daffodils, and hyacinths.) Fill the vase with water to the base of the bulb, and set the bulb in the mouth of the vase. Place it in a cool area until you can see green shoots, then move it to a sunny spot. After the bulb develops roots, keep the water level at the top of the roots to prevent bulb rot. Change the water as necessary to keep it clean. Before you know it, sweetly scented flowers will bloom in your home.

Garden Almanac

■ **Divide peonies.** Peonies, which are best planted in fall, generally thrive for years in the same spot without needing division, but if they bloomed sparsely in spring, it's an indication that the clumps may be overcrowded. Now is also the best time to propagate plants by division, to move clumps that aren't growing well in the site selected, or to relocate specimens that are simply in the wrong place. Lift the plant with as many of the roots intact as possible—established peonies have deep, thick, wide-ranging roots. Carefully remove the soil around the roots, then gently hose the root mass until you see the reddish buds, called eyes, on the crown. Discard old, woody, or rotted portions of the crown, then divide the root mass with a sharp, clean knife, keeping 3 to 5 eyes in each section. Select a site in full sun with well-drained soil, and set them with the eyes facing up, but only 2 inches *below* the soil surface. In warmer areas gardeners plant peonies with the eyes 1 inch deep; if the eyes are any deeper than 2 inches, the plants will not flower. Newly planted divisions bear few flowers the first year, but after 2 or 3 growing seasons, they should bloom prolifically.

■ **Uproot spent annuals and toss them on the compost pile.** Add only plants that are disease-free to the compost pile.

■ **Sow annuals for bloom next year.** Annual poppies such as corn or field poppy (*Papaver rhoeas*) will add sparkling color to sites in full sun next summer if you just take time to scatter some seeds now. Sow forget-me-nots (*Myosotis sylvatica*) in partial shade.

Tulips, like most bulbs, look best planted *en masse*.

■ **Dig tender bulbs when the leaves die back.** In Zone 5, it's still too soon to dig tender bulbs, but farther north, it's time they came inside for storage.

■ **Plant tulips.** Garden centers everywhere abound with spring-blooming bulbs, and any day now the tulips you ordered last month will arrive in your mailbox. Plant tulips as soon as you can after their arrival. While 1 or 2 tulips may bring a hint of color, for maximum impact plant at least 15 of one kind together. Bulbs need excellent

drainage or they will rot. They also need sunlight, which you can find in open areas or under deciduous (leaf-dropping) shrubs and trees, since most tulips bloom early, before the trees leaf out. Concentrate tulips such as Darwin Hybrids or 'Red Emperor' *en masse* around your mailbox to enliven this potentially dull area. Use shorter types, including charming *T. greigii* 'Plaisir', as edgings along a path or near the front of beds and borders. Plant tulip bulbs 6 to 8 inches deep and 5 inches apart.

■ **Move indoors any houseplants that have summered outdoors.** Be sure to bring plants indoors before they can be damaged by early frosts. Inspect plants for signs of insects as you bring them in. To avoid serious pest infestations, treat your houseplants to a thorough spray of horticultural oil, diluted to the growing season ratio, before bringing them indoors for the winter. (Before spraying horticultural oil on the whole plant, test the spray on a couple of leaves and wait a few days to make sure there are no harmful effects.) Or spray with insecticidal soap.

FRUITS AND VEGETABLES

■ **Continue direct-seeding lettuce, endive, escarole, and spinach.** Although the season is drawing to a close, you can sow these crops until mid-September. You'll need to protect any crops sown after that from hard frost later in the season. If you sow seeds in a cold frame or use floating row covers, you can extend the harvest through October and well into November. Plan on 2 or more layers of row covers to provide adequate frost protection.

■ **Harvest the last of your basil before frost.** Basil is damaged by even light frost, so gather the last from the garden before frost threatens. Discard any leaves that appear damaged or diseased.

- **Harvest fall raspberries (*Rubus spp.*).** 'August Red' and 'Fall Red' are exceptionally hardy cultivars that bear September crops. 'Fall Gold' and 'Graton Gold' both bear yellow berries in fall. You may still have blackberries to harvest, too. They aren't as hardy as many raspberries, but 'Arapaho' is an upright thornless cultivar hardy in Zones 5 to 8. Blackberries taste sour when they're glossy black and at their prettiest. They aren't ripe and sweet until they turn dull black.

- **Before a hard frost, harvest fava bean plants.** Pull up entire plants and hang them upside down in a dry, protected place.

- **Begin harvesting cold-tolerant vegetables such as kale and Brussels sprouts.** Since kale tastes sweetest after frost, harvest just a few leaves now. Mulching the kale with a thick layer of leaves or straw

makes it possible to continue harvesting through the late fall and into winter, even with snow on the ground, but leave the central bud at the stem tip intact. Also harvest a few Brussels sprouts, but since these too taste sweeter after frost,

leave most of them for October. Harvest fall crops of peas, which also will survive light frost.

- **Harvest pumpkins and winter squash.** Do this before a hard frost or protect the plants temporarily with a light row cover or old sheet

Mini-pumpkin 'Jack be Little' bears cute, 3- to 4-inch-wide orange fruits that are handsome and long-lasting in holiday decorations. The fruits are edible and sweet-fleshed, too.

to buy them some extra ripening time. Such covers will provide protection to about 27° or 28°F. In the absence of an early hard frost, wait until the pumpkin is fully orange and the stem begins to die before harvesting. To avoid untimely rot, don't scratch a pumpkin when ripe, and harvest pumpkins and winter squash with pruners to keep the stems from breaking off at the base.

■ **Dig up and pot rosemary to overwinter indoors.** Carefully lift the plant from the ground, keeping

as many roots as possible but removing excess soil. Rosemary, native to the warm, sunny, rocky hills around the Mediterranean, needs excellent drainage to keep its roots from rotting. Pot the plants in cactus soil or in a sterile potting soil mixed with extra perlite to promote drainage, and place them near a sunny window with a southern or eastern exposure. Water as necessary, keeping plants neither too wet nor too dry: To judge when to water, stick your index finger about two inches into the soil. If the soil is dry to that depth, then it's time to water. Rosemary dries out easily indoors in central heating; over winter, plants are best kept in a bright, cool spot that stays between 45° and 55°F. To prevent dessication, mist the plants regularly.

■ **Clean up areas of the vegetable garden that have finished producing.** Pull up spent annual herb and vegetable plants, and, if they are disease-free, throw them on the compost pile.

Since rosemary plants resent root disturbance, many northern gardeners keep this popular herb in containers year-round.

  Garden Almanac

*Garden*Bounty

PRESERVING BLACKBERRIES AND RASPBERRIES

Because you don't need to pit or peel blackberries and raspberries, they make excellent candidates for dry-pack freezing, a quick and easy way to preserve food fresh from the garden. To freeze blackberries and raspberries safely and successfully, first pick through them to ensure that you are freezing only fruit of the highest quality. Eat bruised berries right away; don't freeze them. Throw away any berries showing signs of mold, fungus, or other disease. *Do not* wash berries before freezing them, since they can fall apart when wet. Place ripe, firm berries on a cookie sheet so that they are not touching and set the tray in a freezer set to 0°F. As soon as the berries are hard, place them in airtight freezer bags or pack them into clean, dry containers. If you choose the former, carefully compress the bags to remove excess air before sealing and storing.

Ideally, process berries within two hours of harvesting, since the quicker you freeze your fruit, the more successfully it will be preserved. Harvesting and freezing small quantities each day is best, because it reduces the amount of time it takes to freeze the berries. Placing large quantities of unfrozen food in a freezer can slow the freezing process and facilitate the growth of harmful bacteria.

Fall

. . . The startling, fluorescent orange
of a sugar maple shines against
the duller yellow and reddish
purple of mountain ash.
Nights grow longer, days brisk
and scented with wet decaying
leaves. I work in the garden,
surrounded by fiery trees
and a plush carpet of lawn.
Here, at home, lives
Nature in glory.

OCTOBER'S TASKS

THE WHOLE GARDEN
- Have your lawn and garden soil tested at the local Cooperative Extension Service and make recommended improvements.
- Visit garden centers for ideas on fall-blooming plants and bargains.
- Rake up fallen leaves and add them to your compost heap.
- Mulch areas intended for early spring planting.

TREES AND SHRUBS
- Plant bare-root, containerized, and balled-and-burlapped shrubs.
- Transplant established trees and shrubs.
- Water newly planted trees and shrubs deeply before the ground freezes.
- After leaf fall, take hardwood cuttings.

FLOWERS AND GRASSES
- Mow the grass as needed until it stops growing.
- Reseed the lawn until the soil cools.
- Pot up less hardy ornamental grasses.
- Transplant or divide perennials.
- Mark late-to-emerge perennials.
- Cut hardy perennials to the base after fall flowering.
- Clean up your perennial beds.
- Rake up or pull out annuals once they're killed by frost.
- Continue planting hardy spring-flowering bulbs.
- Lift and store tender, summer-flowering bulbs, tubers, and corms.

FRUITS AND VEGETABLES
- Plant garlic all month.
- Plant winter rye for a cover crop.
- Direct-seed lettuce, endive, and escarole.
- Harvest kale and collards all month long.
- Pick mature green tomatoes.
- Take cuttings of your favorite herbs to grow indoors over winter.
- Dig chopped-up leaves into the soil.
- Dig, sever, and replant rooted suckers of raspberries.
- Remove stakes and other garden equipment from the vegetable garden.
- After a killing frost, clean up the vegetable garden.

October's bouquet has an earthy beauty, expressing the transition from late summer's gold and purple flowers to wintry tans and browns. Fall bulbs like meadow saffron (*Colchicum autumnale*) should do well to Zone 4 and add a note of rosy purple or white to a fall nosegay. Likewise, New York and New England asters, along with other late-blooming daisies, bring purple and lilac to the palette, while from southern Zone 5 to Zone 6 you can count on hardy fall repeating roses for both fragrance and poignant charm.

Pee-gee hydrangea (*Hydrangea paniculata* 'Grandiflora') flowerheads make stunning traditional bouquets fresh or dried. Each panicle contains florets ranging in color from rosy pink to cream and soft mossy green. To dry the panicles, cut the stems to the desired length, remove the leaves, and fasten the stems together with a rubber band or string. Hang the heads upside down for 2 or 3 days in a warm, crisp, preferably dark room until dry. Then add them as needed to your fall or winter floral arrangements.

More choices for October bouquets include late-blooming chrysanthemums and the abundantly berried branches of European cranberrybush viburnum (*Viburnum opulus*) or its trouble-free native cousin, American cranberrybush viburnum (*V. trilobum*), which has edible fruits and is hardy to Zone 2. Inflorescences of ornamental grasses add elegance to the fall bouquet. Feather reed grass (*Calamagrostis* × *acutifolia* 'Karl Foerster') has feathery flowers, while the many cultivars of Japanese silver grass (*Miscanthus sinensis*) bear great brushlike plumes that look fabulous alone in a vase or mixed with other plants. Another interesting texture can come in the form of lamb's ears (*Stachys byzantina*), a low-growing, spreading perennial plant with hairy silver leaves. Children and adults find their softness, so similar to puppies' ears, irresistible, and love to touch and stroke them.

1. Tuberose flower.
2. Single Nasturtium.
3. Yellow peren! Poppy.
4. Purple Polyanthos.
5. Saffron flower.
6. Stript! double Colchicum.
7. Single blew Periwinkle.
8. Trumpet flower.
9. Camomile double.
10. Sempervivum Auricula.
11. Indian Tobacco.
12. Arbutus double.
13. Best flowering Geranium.
14. Guernsey Lilly.
15. Autumn Carnation.
16. Agnus Castus.
17. Long blowing Honeysuckle.
18. Pricked Aster.
19. Belladona Lilly.
20. Ever green Honeysuckle.
21. Leonurus or Archangel tree.
22. Black Cranes bill.
23. Scarlet Cranes bill.
24. Marigold tree.
25. Musk Scabious.
26. Double white Musk rose.
27. Box leav'd Myrtle.
28. Michaelmas Daisee.
29. Yellow Passion flower.
30. Hollyhock always doubles.
31. Virginia Shrub Acre.

OCTOBER

From the Collection of Rob! Furber Gardiner at Kensington. 1730.

Design'd by P.r Casteels.

Engrav'd by H. Fletcher.

A garden never sleeps. Something visible or invisible is always happening in the perpetual cycle of growth and decay. This month we do an assortment of tasks aimed at creating next year's garden. We divide and transplant, we harvest, and we tidy up the garden to ensure the healthy and vigorous development of next year's flowers, foods, lawns, and ornamental plants.

THE WHOLE GARDEN

■ **Have your lawn and garden soil tested at the local Cooperative Extension Service and make recommended improvements.** Soil tests analyze your soil and offer individual recommendations for liming and fertilizing your property, leading to more productive soil and healthy lawn, garden, and ornamental plants. You can purchase soil-test kits at a garden center, but your local Cooperative Extension Service can usually perform more extensive analyses, including tests for soil pH, fertility, organic matter, and soluble salts (for gardens where excessive fertilizer use may create a buildup of soluble salts). Take several samples from different areas of the lawn and garden, since soil conditions and requirements may vary throughout the property. To collect a soil sample, first remove mulch or lawn grass and thatch from the area to be tested. With a clean trowel, sampling tube, or spade, collect soil 4 to 5 inches deep in the lawn and 6 to 8 inches down for garden beds and ornamentals. Take 10 samples from different spots in a testing area (like your front lawn) or 5 samples from different locations around the base of a plant or tree. Mix the 10 lawn samples together in a clean bucket, and do the same for sites where ornamentals will be grown. Clean the tool and the bucket after sampling an area to avoid contamination. Place the samples into clean sample bags, which you can obtain from your local Cooperative Extension Service office.

■ **Visit garden centers for ideas on fall-blooming plants and bargains** to see which plants look attractive in your area now. You may discover new plants that last into the fall to prolong your season of bloom, such as white or pink boltonia (*Boltonia asteroides*). Buy healthy plants only.

■ **Rake up fallen leaves and add them to your compost heap** to enrich the mixture. To ensure their rapid decomposition, turn the entire compost pile with a pitchfork. Shredding leaves with a lawn mower before composting speeds the decomposition process. If the leaves are wet, add some sawdust to absorb the excess moisture. Make your compost pile no more than 6 feet high and wide.

■ **Mulch areas intended for early spring planting** with a deep layer of salt hay, straw, shredded leaves, or with black plastic.

Trees and Shrubs

■ **Plant bare-root, containerized, and balled-and-burlapped shrubs.** Fall rains and warm soil temperatures will stimulate healthy root growth, while cool nights will discourage tender vegetative growth that would be killed off in winter. Hold off on planting conifers and broadleaved evergreens until spring.

■ **Transplant established trees and shrubs,** except for conifers and broadleaved evergreens. Remember to dig the new hole before you remove the plant from its old location. The plant should

Pee-gee hydrangea (*Hydrangea paniculata* 'Grandiflora').

be out of the ground for as short a time as possible. Start by exposing the shrub's root area, either by removing or by tying back the bottom branches with twine. With a small shrub, you can proceed to cut the roots around the plant with a spade, leaving as much soil intact as possible. Lift the plant with your spade, place it in its new hole, and backfill the hole with the soil you removed, creating a shallow saucer of soil on the surface for watering. Water deeply after transplanting. Mulch the area to help retain moisture, but keep the mulch at least 3 inches away from the trunk or stems of the plant to avoid crown rot. Do not let the rootball dry out during the transplanting process or afterward. For larger shrubs or trees, dig a trench around the rootball. Then dig under the rootball on each side with a sharp spade. Slide burlap under one side of the plant, then pull it through to the other and

*Garden*Palette

SPECTACULAR FALL COLOR

In my backyard grows a native maple with a nice, shade-giving green canopy. But in October, when the nights are cool and the days are still warm and sunny, that Cinderella tree discards her plain green frock for a queenly gown of brilliant red, orange, and yellow. My tree is *Acer saccharum*, the sugar maple, a key player in northern New England's stunning fall display.

Fall color in the Northeast is the fortuitous result of a distinctive climate favoring the growth of deciduous forests. Yellow, orange, and red leaves come about from changes in light and temperature, although some years the display may be less radiant than others because of temporary shifts in the weather.

Leaves look green when equal amounts of chlorophyll are being produced and broken down within the plant. Chlorophyll helps the tree produce food from sunlight and raw chemicals absorbed by the roots. In autumn, the rate of chlorophyll production and growth slows, causing the leaves of

Garden Almanac

bind with twine. Shift the bound rootball onto a tarp and pull it to the new hole for replanting.

■ **Water newly planted trees and shrubs deeply before the ground freezes.** That's the only way to encourage them to grow vigorous root systems in the initial months after planting.

■ **After leaf fall, take hardwood cuttings** of shrubs, climbers, and roses to propagate them. Fill a pot with moist propagating mix. Make cuttings 4 to 8 inches long from 1-year-old wood, taken from below the stem's terminal bud. Make a straight cut at the top above a leaf node and a slanted cut at the base, just below a node. Insert slanted ends of the cuttings 2 to 4 inches apart in the mix, keeping the top node 1 inch above the surface. Water and place in a sheltered position outside. During the winter, water the cuttings when the soil is not frozen. In late spring, harden off rooted cuttings and move them into the garden.

many trees to brown or yellow. The timely shutdown of chlorophyll production allows yellow pigments that were already present in the leaves to be exposed. Ginkgo (*Ginkgo biloba*, 120 feet high), Norway maple (*Acer platanoides*, 90 feet high), birches (*Betula* spp., up to 90 feet high), European larch (*Larix decidua*, 100 feet high), and golden larch (*Pseudolarix kaempferi*, 120 feet high) are noted for yellow fall color.

Red color comes from an additional pigment produced when leaves store sugars, as those of some maples do, or tannins, in the manner of the oaks. The combination of warm, sunny autumn days and brisk nights below 45°F triggers the production of red pigment in the leaves. Trees with outstanding red to orange fall color include red maple (*Acer rubrum*, 120 feet high), sugar maple (*A. saccharum*, 120 feet high), black tupelo (*Nyssa sylvatica*, 90 feet high), sourwood (*Oxydendron arboreum*, 75 feet high), Korean mountain ash (*Sorbus alnifolia*, 50 feet high), and scarlet or red oak (*Quercus coccinea* or *Q. rubra*, 75 feet high).

Many shrubs and small trees color up well in the fall. Witch hazels (*Hamamelis* spp.) and summersweets (*Clethra* spp.) add shining yellows to the understory, while *Fothergilla* species turn a startling fluorescent orange, making a stunning complement to the yellow autumn leaves of birches and the pinkish to tawny ornamental grasses.

The aptly named burning bush (*Euonymus alata* 'Compacta') turns from medium green to solid fiery red, as do the sumacs (*Rhus* spp.) along highways and scrub lands and in the wilder gardens of the Northeast. Japanese maples (*Acer palmatum*) and their cultivars often look spectacular, with their graceful habit and lacy red fall leaves.

For 3 seasons of beauty, oakleaf hydrangea (*Hydrangea quercifolia*) is unsurpassed. Hardy to Zone 5, it's grown for conical flower panicles in July and handsome oaklike green foliage that turns brilliant red in fall. Native to the southeastern United States, oakleaf hydrangea may die to the ground in winter in Zone 5A and lower. If it does, it will not flower the next summer, since it blooms on old wood. That should not affect its value as a landscape plant since its lush foliage is its primary attribute, and it will survive.

FLOWERS AND GRASSES

- **Mow the grass as needed until it stops growing.** Make the height of the last cut about 2 inches, but be careful not to cut more than ⅓ off the top of the grass blades at any one mowing.

- **Reseed the lawn until the soil cools.** As soil temperature drops, the germination rate of the seed declines. So if you sow your lawn too late in the season for germination to take place,

the seeds will eventually rot in the ground.

- Last chance to **pot up less hardy ornamental grasses** such as fountain grass (*Pennisetum setaceum*) to overwinter in a dry basement or garage that stays above freezing.

Our native boltonia bears white daisies in fall. This is its cultivar 'Pink Beauty'.

- **Transplant or divide perennials** such as daylilies, coral bells, and hostas. After preparing the new site, dig a hole large enough to accommodate the plant with as much of its entire rootball as possible. Lift the plant from its old location and transfer it to the new one. Pat the soil around the plant and water it thoroughly. Divide overgrown clumps as necessary by splitting off portions with healthy young shoots and sufficient roots. Replant the divisions.

- **Mark late-to-emerge perennials** with tags that can withstand winter weather. Plants such as Joe-Pye weed (*Eupatorium* spp.), butterfly weed (*Asclepias tuberosa*), balloon flower (*Platycodon grandiflorus*), and Japanese anemone (*Anemone × hybrida*) come up late in the spring. If their position is not marked, you may forget their location or pull them out, mistaking their young shoots for weeds. Printed plastic tags in potted perennials quickly become brittle and break. Long-lasting aluminum labels cost more than wood and plastic but are worth the extra expense.

- **Cut hardy perennials to the base after fall flowering.** In cold areas, leave about 6 inches of growth on perennials to catch the snow and insulate them from the cold. Cut them all the way back in the spring before growth resumes.

- **Clean up your perennial beds.** Remove dead plant matter that has collected around the base of roses and perennials. Leave plants such as sedum 'Autumn Joy' and

Pennisetum villosum, commonly called feathertop.

ornamental grasses standing for their winter interest.

- **Rake up or pull out annuals once they're killed by frost,** placing them on the compost pile. Throw diseased vegetation in the trash to avoid infecting other plants.

- **Continue planting hardy spring-flowering bulbs** such as daffodils, crocuses, squills, and grape

CREATING A CROCUS FIELD

If you are establishing a new lawn, now is the time to create a crocus field, which will become a vast sea of pastel color in the spring. Buy in bulk a small hardy bulb or corm such as *Crocus tomasinianus*—5,000 corms to cover an 18' × 18' area, 10,000 corms to cover one 30' × 40'. After the topsoil has been spread but before the lawn is seeded, broadcast the tiny corms by hand over the soil. For an attractive, naturalistic appearance, make sure you scatter the corms sparsely around the edges of your asymmetrical drift and densely toward the middle. Spread a thin layer of topsoil over the corms. Seed the lawn, keep it watered, and early the following spring, you'll find your lawn awash in pale lavender. The delicate straplike leaves of the crocus look like grass and thus blend into the lawn. In order to allow the corms to absorb the nourishment necessary for growth, do not mow the grass until the crocus leaves have yellowed.

For the first lawn cutting of the season, set the mower deck at 3 to 4 inches high in order to preserve the crocus foliage as long as possible. Note that *C. tomasinianus* is a prolific sower and will spread in the lawn once planted.

hyacinths in humusy, well-drained soil. The correct planting depth for bulbs varies from 3 to 5 times the height of the bulb, while spacing is 2 to 3 bulb widths apart. Plant bulbs with their roots down and with their pointed growing tips facing up. After digging a hole large enough to plant several bulbs, spread humus or compost in the bottom, set bulbs in place, and cover with soil. Spread a balanced organic fertilizer on the soil surface. You can also layer bulbs for a longer season of bloom by arranging them in tiers according to the correct planting depth of each type. Simply stagger each new layer of bulbs and cover it with soil before planting the next layer. For example, you can combine (from shallow to deep) crocuses, grape hyacinths, and daffodils for an attractive succession and combination of blooms.

■ **Lift and store tender summer-flowering bulbs, tubers, and corms** such as dahlias, cannas, and gladioli when their leaves start to die. Wipe off excess soil and put them in a cool, dry spot with good air circulation. Maintain them over the winter in barely moist peat moss or wood shavings, keeping the air temperature at 40° to 45°F.

FRUITS AND VEGETABLES

■ **Plant garlic all month.** Hard-neck garlic does best in the long, cold winters and short growing season of the Northeast, whereas soft-neck garlic does better in milder climates. Garlic likes good garden soil high in organic matter. For planting, choose bulbs that feel hard, since softness affects the plant's vigor. Pull the bulb apart into individual cloves, being careful not to bruise the cloves with your fingernails or by dropping them. Reject cloves with damaged stems, from which will grow weaker plants. Plant cloves with the blunt stem end downward, and pointed tip up. If you're growing garlic in rows, space the

Garlic flowers appear in summer.

cloves 4 to 6 inches apart and leave room between the rows for you to perform necessary chores like weeding. Plant cloves 2 to 3 inches below the soil surface and cover with a mulch of chopped leaves.

- **Plant winter rye for a cover crop** to protect the soil. Seed it until October 15 in Zones 3 and 4 and November 1 in Zones 5 and 6. Rye chokes out many annual weed seedlings and also helps prevent soil erosion.

- **Direct-seed lettuce, endive, and escarole** in mid-month for fresh greens with your Thanksgiving dinner. Because these plants are susceptible to October frosts, you'll have to grow them in cold frames or under row covers for a late-November harvest.

- **Pick mature green tomatoes** as late in the season as possible and let them ripen indoors. Earlier in the fall, you can cover the plants overnight with burlap to protect them from light frosts. You can see that tomatoes are mature enough to ripen by their shiny, whitish green color and their relative hairlessness compared with immature green tomatoes. Mature green tomatoes will ripen in darkness at room temperature; they don't need to sit on a

windowsill. Or, consider uprooting your plants before frost and ripening the fruit on the plants on a hook in your garage or basement.

- **Take cuttings of your favorite herbs to grow indoors over winter.** Or dig up whole herb plants, trim them, and pot them in potting soil mix to use indoors. Sage, scented geraniums, basil, and chives are among the plants that thrive indoors. Leaving dead leaves on perennial herbs left outdoors helps protect them in colder areas.

To discourage fungal diseases, pick or rake leaves and fallen debris off low-growing evergreen herbs such as thyme.

- **Dig chopped-up leaves into the soil** for a healthy dose of rich organic matter that will decompose over the winter.

- **Dig, sever, and replant rooted suckers of raspberries** to propagate the plants. If any leaves remain on the plant, remove and discard them to keep your garden healthy.

- **Remove stakes and other garden equipment from the vegetable garden,** wash them thoroughly, dry with a cloth or in the sun, and store for the winter.

- **After a killing frost, clean up the vegetable garden.** Remove all dead or half-dead plants to the compost pile, avoiding root vegetables that are still in the garden. Make sure you throw diseased plants into the trash; this is crucial for your soil's health. Turn the soil in those vegetable beds that are now empty, incorporating aged manure and compost into the earth.

Rose hips and other fall fruits add color to the garden and are food for wildlife.

Garden Almanac

*Garden*Bounty

VERSATILE ROSE HIPS

All roses bear fruits known as hips, some of which can color the autumn garden. For example, rugosa rose (*Rosa rugosa*) and some of its cultivars (most notably 'Frau Dagmar Hartopp'), produce inch-wide hips that look like fat red tomatoes, while *R. glauca* is known for its purplish leaves and abundant fruit shaped like small, bright red bottles.

Even roses with less showy fruit are worth growing. Shining rose (*R. nitida*) grows wild from Newfoundland to Connecticut and bears red hips less than a half-inch wide. While gardeners appreciate its 2-foot-high stature, its bright rosy pink flowers, and the scarlet fall color of its shiny leaves, birds such as robins, bobwhites, ruffed grouse, and ring-necked pheasants feast on its red hips.

People also eat rose hips, a proven source of Vitamin C. Hips from *R. rugosa* and dog rose (*R. canina*) taste good in teas, jams, and jellies. Hips are ready to harvest when their color deepens and they look full and ripe. For rose hip tea, first wash the hips and dry them in a single layer in a warm, dark, dry room. When completely dry, chop them finely in a blender or food processor and store the pieces in a tightly sealed glass jar in a dark cupboard. To brew, steep one teaspoon of powdered hips for 5 minutes in a cup of boiling water. Avoid consuming rose hips from plants treated with toxic chemicals.

Ripened hips of shrub rose 'Country Dancer'.

THE WHOLE GARDEN

- Mark your paths and driveway with stakes.
- Store firewood outdoors.
- Clean, oil, and sharpen your garden tools.
- Prepare the lawn mower for winter storage.
- Adjust soil pH, if necessary.
- Before the ground freezes hard, install bluebird nesting boxes.

TREES AND SHRUBS

- Make sure all leaves are off your lawns before heavy snows begin.
- Spray antidessicants on broadleaved evergreens.
- Water broadleaved evergreens on warm days.
- Fertilize trees and shrubs when dormant.

FLOWERS AND GRASSES

- Keep planting daffodil bulbs until the ground freezes.
- Finish cutting back perennials.
- Mulch perennial gardens once the ground has frozen.

FRUITS AND VEGETABLES

- Continue harvesting kale and collards until snow is on the ground.
- Harvest greens in your cold frame for Thanksgiving dinner.
- Finish putting the garden to bed.

Furber's November bouquet must diverge from mine because of differences in climate. While flowers are still growing in England, my garden is quiet. The asters and coneflowers have faded. In a warm fall, there may be a lingering goldenrod by the roadside, reblooming lavender and delphinium in my flowerbed, and one or two marigolds on the south side of the house. American cranberrybush viburnum (*Viburnum trilobum*) still has clusters of succulent, edible, red berries on its stems, and the fruit of linden viburnum (*V. dilatatum*) stays bright red through December. Viburnum stems, together with branches of bittersweet (*Celastrus scandens*), make a lovely seasonal display for a vase or centerpiece.

One friend of mine, looking to add bittersweet's bold orange-and-red berries to her Thanksgiving centerpiece, scavenged through brush and trees in a neighbor's yard looking for perfect, berry-filled branches. She found them, and her table that year was glorious. Her hands,

mber

however, scabbed and bleeding with poison ivy from the hunt, were not. When flowers fade and you begin to look beyond your immediate garden for brilliant berries, curling stems, curious seedpods, and wafting plumes, be aware of your surroundings. Even when those shiny triptychs of leaves are not visible on the plant, you can contract poison ivy from the twining woody vine itself.

While poison ivy is hazardous to touch, many other plants are toxic only when ingested. Keep small children and pets away from bittersweet because it is poisonous. Similarly, if your dog is a digger, know that daffodil bulbs contain a potentially deadly alkaloid. This foul poison protects the bulbs by making their taste repugnant to people, animals, and most other pests. Many of the broadleaved evergreens that adorn holiday tables are also toxic if eaten, including rhododendrons, boxwood, mountain laurels (*Kalmia* spp.), and the ground cover English ivy.

1 Ficoides or fig Marigold.
2 White Perewinkle.
3 Curleos flowering Launstinus.
4 Blew Perewinkle.
5 Tree Candy tuft.
6 Umbrouden'd Cranes bill.
7 Yellow-michl Eternal.
8 Arop'd single Anemone.
9 Borage.
10 Thyme leav'd Myrtle.
11 French Marigold.
12 Colchicum, Autumna major.
13 Ilex leav'd Jasmines.
14 Great purple Cranos bill.
15 Arbutus or Strawberry tree.
16 Double Nasturtium.
17 Broad leav'd red Valerian.
18 Myrtos Cistus.
19 Virginian Aster.
20 Campanula Canariensis.
21 Pheasants Eye.
22 Perennial dwarf Sun flower.
23 Double Featherfew.
24 Carolina Star flower.
25 Scarlet Althæa.
26 Spanish white Jasmine.
27 Lavender with divided Leaves.
28 Golden Rod.
29 American Viburnum.
30 Yellow Dwarf Aloe.
31 Single flow. Anemone.
32 Purple Ficoides.
33 Groundsell tree.
34 Pellitory with Bay flowers.
35 Scarlet single Anemone.
36 White Bryum holly hock.
37 Caper Bush.
38 Dwarf Colutea.

NOVEMBER

Design'd by P.r Casteels.

From the Collection of Rob.t Furber Gardner at Kensington 1730.

Engrav'd by H. Fletcher.

Trees bare of leaves reveal the beauty of bark. Birches stand out, with papery snow-white trunks and branches or peeling layers of salmon bark. Silvery beech bark is smooth, hard, and unblemished. The golden European ash (*Fraxinus excelsior* 'Aurea') reaches skyward, its yellow shoots and golden branches contrasting with black velvet buds. Nature's sweeping arm transforms my garden from its blazing fall glory into a cooler, subtler space.

The Whole Garden

- **Mark your paths and driveway with stakes.** Do this job before the ground freezes. Stakes will make it easier to see where to shovel and plough snow without harming your lawn and flowerbeds.

- **Store firewood outdoors.** Insects hidden under the bark or inside the log will emerge indoors when they are exposed to warm temperatures.

- **Clean, oil, and sharpen your garden tools.** The flip side to the joy of owning a plethora of tools is the effort required to maintain them in top condition. They must be cleaned—if not after each use then at least at the end of each season. First scrape loose dirt from spade, shovel, and knife blades, as well as from the tines of rakes and garden forks. Rinse the tools with a hose and set them in the sun against a building to dry. If you see rust spots, scrub them off with a wire brush. Then rub the blades or tines with vegetable oil to preserve them and keep them from rusting. Sharpen spades, knives, and pruners. Resolve to clean your tools after each use next year, since dirty tools encourage the spread of soil-borne disease from plant to plant.

- **Prepare the lawn mower for winter storage.** Drain the gas tank or, preferably, add a gas stabilizer to a full tank and run the motor for five minutes prior to winter storage. Sharpen or replace the blade, clean dirt and grass from the underside of the mower to prevent rust, change the oil, and clean the air filter.

■ **Adjust soil pH, if necessary.** If you sent soil samples off for testing last month, you'll probably have results back. The pH of your soil will be indicated, along with recommendations for adjusting it. Lawn grasses and many perennials grow best in slightly acid to neutral soil, with a pH of roughly 6.5 to 7.0. If you live in the eastern half of the United States, where soil tends to be acidic—also called sour—you may need to raise the pH with an occasional application of lime. In the western states alkaline, or sweet, soils are common, and sulfur is used to lower their pH. One good reason to test the soil in different parts of your yard separately is that the pH may vary from spot to spot, and the ideal pH for the plants you want to grow there will vary as well. Fall is a good time to lower soil pH by spreading lime, because freezing and thawing in winter and early spring help break the lime down and into the ground.

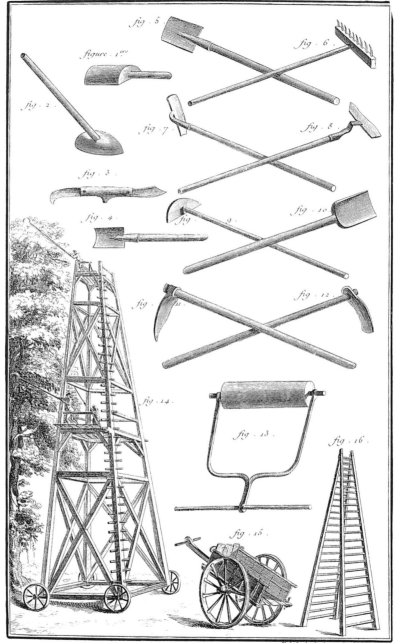

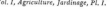

Birds and Bees

BIRDHOUSES FOR YOUR GARDEN

If you have bluebirds living in your yard, you are sharing in one of the true joys of gardening. At least, that's how my husband and I feel now that Eastern bluebirds breed in the nesting box we put up. Their beauty and nonstop activity transfix us, changing the rhythm of our lives as we anticipate the flow of days they spend with us. We are no longer alone in the garden. The female carries pine needles and dry grasses to build a nest. The male protects her while she warms the eggs and waits for them to hatch; once hatched, the babies' demand for food keeps both parents hopping.

In the North, bluebirds usually arrive in mid-March, when the ground is still frozen. Thus, if you'd like bluebirds in your garden next spring, install nesting boxes now, while the ground is soft enough to dig holes for posts to mount them on. You can also mount houses on fenceposts or even a lone tree that lacks lower branches. Bluebirds prefer nesting boxes that are mounted with the bottom of the box 3 to 5 feet above the ground.

Bluebirds aren't difficult to please, but by selecting a suitable spot for the boxes you can increase your chances of hosting a family of them next season. They require open land around their nesting boxes—a box mounted in the lawn or an area of low-mown meadow is ideal—and will generally shun boxes mounted next to dense cover. They do appreciate having places to perch nearby, such as posts, shrubs, or trees. Our T-shaped post, which holds raspberry support wires in place, works well because it also gives the bluebirds a perch. From here they scout the lawn and garden beds for insects. Fledglings use the perch for a rest stop on early forays away from the nest. We attached our box to the outside of the post, facing the open, sunny lawn. About 15 yards away, on the other side of the post, is the edge of the woods, with white pines and a few young sugar maples.

American Song Birds THE BLUEBIRD

3/5 SIZE

NAT. SIZE

© S. M. Co.

To keep bluebirds healthy and maintain their food supply, avoid using insecticides and herbicides.

Bluebirds are territorial, so site boxes at least 100 yards away from each other. Fortunately, while they don't want other bluebirds within 100 yards of their nesting box, bluebirds tolerate other species nearby. Take advantage of their forbearance by installing more houses and creating a garden just for the birds. See "Houses for Birds" on page 19 for suggestions on mounting boxes to keep out predators, as well as for details on what size entrance hole you'll need; different sizes attract different species of birds. Boxes should open on either the top or the side to make them easy to clean. In late winter or autumn, clean the inside, wearing rubber gloves. Remove old nests, discarding them far from the box to discourage the birds from reusing pest-infested materials. Unclog drainage holes and rinse the box with water. Recheck the box in early spring to make sure no other critters have moved in.

Once nesting activity begins in spring, you may want to monitor your boxes by opening them every few days. This discourages other birds—especially house sparrows—from building in them. House sparrows compete heavily with bluebirds for nesting space. Bluebirds build a loosely cup-shaped nest consisting of dry grass, pine needles, weed stems, tiny twigs, and sometimes feathers. The nest is lined with finer materials. House sparrows, on the other hand, generally build a rounded, somewhat messy nest that often contains bits of paper, string, or cloth. Their nests are lined with hair, feathers, or other materials. Discard house sparrow nests promptly to try to discourage them. (If you're unsure of the identity of the nest-builder, watch the box to see who goes in and out.) In spring, we sometimes discard 1 or 2 sparrow nests before they get discouraged and bluebirds can move in.

Several other charming birds commonly build nests in bluebird boxes. Leave their nests in place and enjoy them. You also may want to install nesting boxes especially designed for these species.

House wrens build rounded nests consisting mostly of twigs, small stems, and leaves. The nest is lined with soft material such as feathers. These birds often fill their houses right to the top with nesting materials.

Chickadees construct a cup-shaped nest with a base made of moss. The nest itself consists of fiber, hair, feathers, and plant down.

Tufted titmice also form a cup-shaped nest with a moss base, but they generally incorporate dead leaves. The cup-shaped portion consists of fur, hair, and various fibers such as wool or cotton.

Nuthatches line the floors of their nesting boxes with flakes of bark or small chunks of earth, then form a cup with finely shredded bark, grass, and small roots. The nest is lined with fur, wool, and hair or feathers.

Tree swallows build their nests out of materials such as dry grass and pine needles and line the cup, where the eggs are laid, with feathers.

TREES AND SHRUBS

■ **Make sure all leaves are off your lawns before heavy snows begin.** Matted leaves will smother the lawn and kill it. You can rake them off by hand, which is great exercise, or try using a bagging lawn mower and simply mow them up. Leaves collected with a bagging mower are chopped up and ready to use as mulch next year—add them to your compost pile, or use them to cover empty beds in the flower and vegetable garden.

■ **Spray antidessicants on broadleaved evergreens.** Plants lose water through their leaves in a process called transpiration. Deciduous trees shed their foliage in fall, which reduces the amount of moisture they lose; but evergreens continue losing water through their leaves all winter long. If they lose too much, their leaves will turn brown and they may die. Frozen soil and drought aggravate water loss by preventing

Pl. II.

H." Redouté del.'

Renard sc.

ILEX opaca.

the roots from taking up water from the earth. Drying winds also contribute to this condition, which is called winterburn. Evergreens planted on south-facing sites are most susceptible to winterburn; when their leaves heat up on sunny winter days while the soil is still frozen, the plants can't replace the water lost. To reduce moisture loss and help prevent winterburn, protect the leaves of evergreens such as hollies, mountain laurel, and many rhododendrons with an antidessicant spray, available at garden centers. Apply the spray when the temperature is above freezing, so that the water in the waxy solution can evaporate and the wax can coat the leaf.

■ **Water broadleaved evergreens on warm days.** Because broadleaved evergreens lose water through their leaves all winter, water them when the temperature rises to approximately 40°F.

■ **Fertilize trees and shrubs when dormant.** If you live in a climate where the ground freezes solid, your shrubs may benefit from an application of nitrogen. Fertilizing now encourages abundant root growth, which will go on for weeks after the top growth has ceased.

Digging In

PROTECTING ROSES FOR WINTER

Many popular roses aren't hardy in northern zones and require protection to survive the winter. To protect a rose in a cold climate, first remove any remaining leaves from the plant and from the ground to avoid spreading fungal diseases. If you use chemicals in your garden, spray the beds and bushes with fungicide. For hardy shrub roses and old garden roses such as albas, damasks, and gallicas, after a hard freeze mound fresh soil (not from your rose bed), compost, or well-rotted manure 8 to 12 inches high over the base of the plants. Mulching too early stimulates new shoot growth, thus slowing dormancy. For hybrid teas, grandifloras, floribundas, and less hardy old garden roses, first make a chicken-wire cage for the plant by pounding stakes well into the ground around the plant and then wrapping chicken wire around them. Mound the soil or compost over the base of the rose, then fill the cage with straw, leaves, or pine needles. In place of a cage, you can lay pine boughs or other loose mulches over the compost mound.

Styrofoam rose cones, another form of protection suitable for smaller cultivars, are available from catalogues and garden centers. To install a rose cone, prune the canes of your rose bush, tie them together, and fit them under the cone so that the cone sits flat on the ground. Weight the cone down and make 4 pencil-size holes around the top for air circulation. Winter care for climbers includes mounding soil or compost over the crown of the plant and securing canes to their support with rope or heavy twine. In very cold climates, tie canes together and wrap them in burlap.

David Austin English shrub rose 'Lillian Austin'.

■ **Keep planting daffodil bulbs until the ground freezes.** Although the best time to plant daffodil bulbs is earlier in the autumn, you can keep planting them until the ground freezes. Bulbs planted late will still flower the following season, but they will not develop as large a root system as bulbs planted in mid-fall.

■ **Finish cutting back perennials** unless you're preserving them for winter interest. If you have plants with forms that add nothing to the beauty of your winter garden, cut them to a height of 3 to 6 inches, depending on the size of the mature plant, so that the dead foliage won't harbor insects over the winter.

■ **Mulch perennial gardens once the ground has frozen.** Cover plantings of perennials with a 3- to 6-inch layer of compost. Make sure to keep the compost away from the crowns of the plants, as it will cause rot. This topping acts as winter protection and as an organic fertilizer to boost spring growth in your garden. For further protection, spread some chopped leaves over the compost, topped with a layer of evergreen boughs. The leaves and boughs insulate the plants and help prevent heaving during cycles of freezing and thawing.

*Garden*Magic

SAVING PERENNIALS FOR WINTER INTEREST

The stems and seedheads of some perennials add lacy texture, subtle color, and pleasing silhouettes to your landscape all winter long, especially when highlighted against the snow. Weak-stemmed perennials that will be flattened to the ground at the first snowfall are best cut back in fall, but perennials with sturdy stems can be left standing until late winter. Few perennials are as sturdy as sedum 'Autumn Joy', which remains erect and shrubby through most of the winter. Its masses of flattish seedheads, the color of unsweetened chocolate, serve as a reminder of the dormant garden underneath the snow. Anise hyssop (*Agastache foeniculum*) also stands reliably through the winter months. It forms a rounded, 4-foot-high mass of vertical stems topped with dark tan seedheads that stick up like a spiky crewcut. The dense,

blackish, somewhat conical seedheads of coneflowers—including purple coneflowers (*Echinacea purpurea*) and orange coneflowers (*Rudbeckia* spp.)—also add winter interest, and birds love to feast on the seedheads. Towering great coneflower (*R. maxima*) and *R. nitida* 'Herbstsonne', at about 6 and 7 feet tall respectively, add an architectural quality to the winter garden. In my Zone 5 garden, butterfly bush (*Buddleia davidii*) acts like a perennial, since it dies to the ground each winter. Fortunately, it leaves a fine brown fountain of stems and

pointed terminal seedheads to enjoy during the winter months. *B. davidii* 'Pink Delight' is particularly elegant in winter because its seedheads are larger, denser, and more shapely than those of other cultivars. Many ornamental grasses also have a graceful presence in winter, their seedheads ranging from majestic plumes to little hanging capsules resembling fairy lanterns.

Ornamental grasses offer reliable winter interest, too. Large clumps of *Miscanthus sinensis*, sometimes called Japanese silver grass, add fountains of fine-textured, buff-tan foliage to the landscape all winter. Shrub-size cultivars such as 'Gracillimus' or 'Morning Light', which form vase-shaped clumps that reach 5 feet high and wide, make handsome additions to large gardens. Where space is a problem, try slightly smaller 'Yaku Jima', which ranges from 3 to 4 feet. *Pennisetum alopecuroides* 'Hameln', at 1½ to 2 feet is another good choice for small space gardeners. It also doesn't self-sow, a problem exhibited by its parent species.

If you would like to add a somewhat more formal, structured look to your beds and borders in winter—and eye-catching color in summer—consider installing pillars or obelisks. Enjoy the snow-topped structures through the winter, then decorate them with annual vines for summertime.

FRUITS AND VEGETABLES

■ **Harvest greens in your cold frame for Thanksgiving dinner.** By installing electric heating cables in a bed of sand at the bottom of the cold frame, you may be able to extend your harvest beyond Thanksgiving. Keep an eye on the temperature inside cold frames, especially on warm, sunny days when they can heat up quickly. An automatic venting arm (available through garden supply catalogues) is a great investment, since it will open the lid for you when temperatures rise.

■ **Finish putting the garden to bed.** Check to be sure you've removed all the stakes and other equipment from the garden. If you didn't turn the soil in October, spread a 3- to 6-inch layer of compost topped by chopped leaves over the garden to add organic matter for next year.

THE WHOLE GARDEN

■ Save wood ashes from the fireplace or wood stove for soil amendment.

■ Continue to weed until the first snow falls.

■ Apply winter mulches after the ground has frozen.

■ Bring clay pots and statues made of cement, clay, and some resins indoors.

■ Stock up on sand or kitty litter to cope with icy paths.

TREES AND SHRUBS

■ Water evergreens, especially newly planted ones, when the ground is not frozen.

■ Arrange for winter tree pruning.

■ Prepare for a live Christmas tree now.

■ Protect shrubs planted under your roofline from snow damage.

■ Check for mole tunnels and fill them with soil before the ground freezes.

FLOWERS AND GRASSES

■ Continue starting paperwhites every few weeks for nonstop indoor bloom.

■ Start seeds of biennial flowers that you want to treat as annuals.

■ Water houseplants thoroughly, but not too frequently.

■ Treat your houseplants to pebble trays.

■ Stop feeding houseplants.

FRUITS AND VEGETABLES

■ Mulch strawberries to insulate them from cycles of freezing and thawing.

■ Cut fall-bearing raspberries to the ground.

■ Harvest herbs indoors.

December bouquets needn't be limited to a mass of seasonal greens. Creating the dynamic effect of Furber's exotic arrangement, full of contrasting shapes, textures, and colors, is as easy as a trip to the flower shop. Even supermarkets carry a fascinating variety of exotic flowers and plants to be combined for dramatic effect. In fact, flowering pot plants such as cyclamen, kalanchoes, poinsettias (especially ones grown in very small pots), gloxinias, and primroses are stunning arranged with a mix of greens. For a more exotic touch, consider using bromeliads, orchids, or even stately amaryllis. To make watering easy and to protect your furniture, build arrangements on a table pad or other waterproof surface, then set all the pots in good-sized waterproof saucers. (If you're using small pots, a single large saucer makes watering especially easy and foolproof.) Cover up the saucer and surround the pots with greens. Then add pinecones, ribbon, ornaments, or other accessories to suit your style.

After poinsettias, florist's cyclamen (*Cyclamen persicum*) are among the most popular flowering plants of the season. These beauties bear heart-shaped dark green leaves patterned with silver and flowers with twisted petals in clear white, pink, purple, or red. While *C. persicum* isn't hardy outdoors north of Zone 9, plants require cool temperatures to grow well: Keep them in a spot where temperatures range from 45° to 50°F at night and no more than 68°F during the daytime. If given cool conditions, the plants prefer bright sunlight; set them away from direct light if you can't give them the chilly conditions they prefer. Don't overlook the miniature cyclamen sometimes offered alongside larger florist types. About ⅛ the size of their larger cousins, they come in the same colors and are commonly sold in 3-inch pots. Since they grow better at warmer temperatures than florist types, they are better choices for growing indoors. Set on a bright windowsill and watered regularly, pots of miniature cyclamen will bloom continuously until spring. Their small pots also make them especially easy to add to table arrangements.

1 Royal purple Auricula.
2 African white flower'd Heath.
3 Pansies or Hearts ease.
4 White Corn Marigold.
5 Strawberry daisie.
6 Cape Marigold.
7 Shining leav'd Laurustinus.
8 Marye du Mond Auricula.
9 Red spring Cyclamen.
10 White Cyclamen.
11 Yellow Ficoides.
12 Yellow round Eternal.
13 Christmas flower.
14 Winter white Primrose.
15 Gentianella.
16 Yellow Corn Marigold.
17 Scarlet Geranium.
18 Canary Pellitory.

DECEMBER

19 Valerianella.
20 Winter double Cromfoot.
21 Strip'd leav'd Geranium.
22 Cape Marigold white within.
23 St. Peters Herb.
24 Mountain Avens.
25 Single purple Anemone.
26 Sage & Rosemary tree.
27 Winter wall flower.
28 Winter flowering Pear.
29 Lavender lav'd Groundsel tree.
30 Scarlet African Aloe, with Pyramidal Leaves.
31 Spanish Virgins bower.
32 Glastenbury thorne.
33 Rue in plane.
34 Bauhelia.
35 Monthly rose bud.
36 Trifid African golden knot.

Design'd by Mr. Casteels.

From the Collection of Rob.t Furber gardiner at Kensington. 1730.

Engrav'd by H. Fletcher.

S now and the holidays go hand in hand. The earth's transformation from brown, green, and dirty purple to the clarity of white excites me. On a clear night with a full moon, the garden takes on magical proportions. Dry stone walls appear antediluvian, remnants of a prehistoric age. Moonlight magnifies every tree and turns the landscape blue.

THE WHOLE GARDEN

- **Save wood ashes from the fireplace or wood stove for soil amendment.** Wood ashes are an organic source of potash, or potassium, which—along with nitrogen and phosphorus—is an important component of most fertilizers. Amending your soil with wood ashes also raises the pH, making the soil more alkaline (less acid). Wood ashes work faster than lime and should be applied no more than once every 2 or 3 years at a rate of 25 pounds per 1,000 square feet. You can also add wood ashes to the compost pile.

- **Continue to weed until the first snow falls.** If you're consistent with weeding, you'll save yourself an unthinkable amount of back-breaking work in the spring.

- **Apply winter mulches after the ground has frozen.** Don't mulch before the ground freezes, or you'll make a warm, cozy home for mice and other creatures to move in and feed on plant roots and crowns. Salt marsh hay, oak leaves, pine needles, and straw are all effective—and convenient, too—since they will not mat over winter. Maple leaves, on the other hand, will mat down and smother or rot plants underneath them; don't mulch with them unless they've been finely chopped in a leaf shredder or a bagging lawn mower.

- **Bring clay pots and statues made of cement, clay, and some resins indoors.** Repeated freezing and thawing will crack these garden objects, so they should be stored indoors. Be sure to clean them before moving them inside. If items are too heavy to move, cover them with a tarp or plastic to keep them dry over winter. When potting up plants to keep outdoors through the winter, use a layer of about ⅓ Styrofoam shipping peanuts at the bottom of the pot, rather than terra-cotta pot shards, to help keep the pots from cracking. Top with two-thirds Pro-mix potting soil.

- **Stock up on sand or kitty litter to cope with icy paths.** These materials are good alternatives to salt, which hinders the intake of water through the roots of plants, and could destroy your lawn and any nearby shrubs and trees through drought stress. If you want to melt the ice, calcium chloride is less damaging to the environment than sodium chloride.

TIP: Styrofoam shapes covered with juniper greens and other decorative elements make foolproof outdoor arrangements to adorn this stone wall at Fenimore Art Museum in Cooperstown, New York. Good drainage is essential, as water freezing in the pots will break them.

TREES AND SHRUBS

■ **Arrange for winter tree pruning.** Talk to your arborist now about large trees on your property that will need pruning before spring. You may be able to negotiate a better rate for pruning now, because crews are not as busy as they will be come spring. Arrange to have trees pruned sometime over the winter, as weather permits.

■ **Prepare for a live Christmas tree now.** It's nice to be able to enjoy the tree you get for Christmas after the holiday is over. If possible, dig a hole to plant your tree early in the month, before the ground has frozen; then fill the hole with leaves and cover the pile of removed soil with a tarp.

Why not decorate a live tree to bring the Christmas spirit to your garden?

Once you bring your live tree home, keep it indoors for no more than 3 to 5 days. Remember, the longer a tree stays indoors, the less it will be able to readjust to the cold temperatures and conditions outdoors. Plant the tree in your predug hole as soon as possible, water deeply, and spray with an antidessicant. If you can't plant immediately, or need to store the tree for any length of time, move it to an unheated space, spray with an antidessicant, and keep the root ball from drying out. If you don't have a predug hole and the ground is too frozen for planting, make sure the root ball stays damp and cool until the spring thaw.

■ **Protect shrubs planted under your roofline from snow damage.** Stake and wrap shrubs with burlap or cover them with a wooden A-frame. For the health of the plants and for your own convenience, transplant them in spring to a location away from the roofline.

■ **Check for mole tunnels and fill them with soil before the ground freezes.** This will help protect plant roots from damage caused by the freezing and thawing of water that has accumulated inside the holes.

DECK THE HALLS

If you want to deck your halls with boughs of holly or other evergreens, by all means take pruners in hand. But when cutting greens for seasonal decoration, keep in mind that you are pruning. Make cuts over the entire plant, rather than concentrating on one area. You will have to live with the results of your pruning for years to come, so try to maintain a balanced, shapely appearance with each plant; it's a good idea to step back periodically and examine the plant from all sides. Make proper pruning cuts, cutting branches back to another branch, or to just above a bud or shoot pointing in the direction in which you want growth to go.

If you traditionally cut greens for the holidays, make sure that any pruning you do earlier in the season is light enough to allow for a further trim in December. If you're tempted to prune hollies before December, don't! Fall—late August through November—is the time for hollies to harden off and go into dormancy, a winter resting period when no growth occurs. Fall-pruned hollies can develop tender new growth, making the plant susceptible to winter damage.

Evergreen wreaths, swags, garlands, and kissing balls last much longer outdoors than in. If you want to use them indoors, you might treat them with a clear plastic spray, available at craft stores, to preserve the leaves and keep the plants glossy. Add pinecones and twigs of winterberry to your designs. Give a merry look to empty window boxes by filling them with greens, cones, and berried stems.

You can create stunning, long-lasting arrangements either for outdoors or in by covering styrofoam forms with prunings from various evergreens plus pinecones, seedpods, and other natural materials. This wreath at Fenimore Art Museum in Cooperstown, New York, is covered with juniper and boxwood trimmings, plus dried cockscomb flowers (*Celosia* spp.). To insert prunings and other decorations easily into the styrofoam, wire them to wooden floral picks (available at craft stores). Since these decorations are lightweight, be sure to fasten them securely or they will blow over in winter winds.

POINSETTIAS

Poinsettias, those ubiquitous red-and-green holiday plants, don't look quite so traditional any more. Yes, big, showy red ones abound, but new colors and forms make poinsettia picking more fun. Solid colors available now include white, pink, peach, coral, and yellow.

'Winter Rose' has curly dark red bracts resembling fully double, velvety red roses, and dark green leaves. 'Jingle Bells' has light red bracts marked with white, while 'Candy Cane' has white bracts speckled with pink or red. Pink 'Silverbells' has white marbled variegation on

bracts and leaves, while 'Monet Twilight' is multi-toned, ranging from palest pink on the lower bracts to deep rose at the top.

These tender perennials, hardy from Zone 9 south, bear insignificant, greenish white flowers in flat flowerheads that are surrounded by big bracts—actually modified leaves. The plant is named for Joel Robert Poinsett, a southern plantation owner, botanist, and the first U.S. ambassador to Mexico (1825 to 1829). These native Mexican shrubs, in bloom from late autumn to spring, so delighted Ambassador Poinsett that he sent several of them to his South Carolina plantation, where they thrived in the greenhouse. Their botanical name, *Euphorbia pulcherrima*, refers to *pulcher*, the Latin word for *beautiful*.

When choosing a poinsettia, look for a full, shapely plant with dense foliage all down the stem. Ideally, the plant should be 2½ times taller than the diameter of the pot. Skip plants with wilted leaves and wet soil—a sign of possible root rot. Be careful with plants in plastic or paper sleeves, since these packagings can cramp and damage the branches. However, it may be necessary to give your poinsettia some protection—a grocery bag will do—on the way home from the store, since wind and temperatures below 50°F can also hurt it.

Inside your home, poinsettias prefer indirect or diffuse sunlight for at least 6 hours a day. Place them away from drafts of cold or hot air, and maintain a daytime temperature no warmer than 70°F. Moisten the soil by watering the pot thoroughly when the surface feels dry. Never let poinsettias sit in water, however, or they could die from root rot. Do not fertilize them once they bloom.

If you're game for a challenge, keep a poinsettia after the holiday and bring it into bloom the following year. In late March or early April, cut the plant to about 8 inches high to stimulate May growth. Your poinsettia needs indirect sun and regular watering even when not in bloom. Place plants outdoors once night temperatures are at least 55°F. During spring, summer, and fall, fertilize your poinsettia every 2 to 3 weeks. In June, repot plants that have outgrown their containers, using potting soil rich in peat moss or another form of organic matter. Keep your plant bushy and compact during the summer by pruning or pinching, but stop cutting it back after September 1.

At summer's end, bring your plant indoors. Lengthening autumn nights trigger bud set and flower production in poinsettias. For your poinsettia to rebloom, you must keep it in total darkness for 14 hours each night beginning October 1. Placing a large box over the plant at night helps prevent stray light from disturbing the process. To bring on flowering, the poinsettia needs 6 to 8 hours of bright sunlight daily, and 60° to 70°F evening temperatures throughout October, November, and early December. Keep watering and fertilizing regularly, and after 8 to 10 weeks your poinsettia will bloom again.

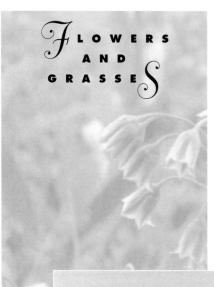

FLOWERS AND GRASSES

- **Start seeds of biennial flowers that you want to treat as annuals.** Biennials sown now insist on flowering the first year.

- **Water houseplants thoroughly, but not too frequently.** In midwinter you should increase the number of days between waterings, but keep the amount of water applied at each watering constant. Houseplants grow slowly in winter, and too much soil moisture can cause root rot.

- **Treat your houseplants to pebble trays.** To create a more humid environment for your plants, place them on pebble-lined trays filled with water. Make sure the pots remain above the level of the water. Central heating dries out the atmosphere of your house, so keep your humidifiers clean and filled with water.

- **Stop feeding houseplants.** Start feeding them again when new growth begins in late February.

TIP: Corms of florist's cyclamen or sowbread (*Cyclamen persicum*) that have flowered can bloom again the next year. Let them rest over the summer, watering them rarely and stopping all fertilizer applications. Renew regular watering and fertilizing in the early fall. If you repot your cyclamen, use well-drained sterile potting medium and keep the top of the corm above the soil. Blooming pots of sowbread look jolly in a basket, along with pinecones or oranges.

FRUITS AND VEGETABLES

- **Mulch strawberries to insulate them from cycles of freezing and thawing.** Protect the plants with pine boughs or a 3-inch layer of straw or salt hay once the ground has frozen.

- **Cut fall-bearing raspberries to the ground.** Fall-bearing raspberries are the easiest of the brambles to prune; all you need to do is to cut the canes back to ground level. Don't leave stubs, because these will grow into weak, spindly, unproductive canes next season.

- **Harvest herbs indoors.** Pinch sprigs off herbs overwintering on your windowsill to add a taste of the garden to soups and salads.

Birds and Bees

American Song Birds   Rose-Breasted Grosbeak

NAT. SIZE

½ SIZE

J.L. Ridgway

© S. M. Co.

In the spirit of holiday giving, why not remember the birds by installing a feeder and keeping it filled with food? Birds awaken us in the morning with song; they keep us glued to the windows with their antics; they reflect Nature's infinite substance and diversity.

To attract the widest variety of birds, plan on offering a smörgasbord in several different types of feeders. Filling feeders year-round makes your garden extra bird-friendly, as does planting berry-bearing shrubs. Often the birds attracted to your feeders will also eat insects when available and will help keep down the pest population in your garden come summer.

Sunflower seeds are a great favorite and, together with white proso millet, are the backbone of a good feeding program. Black oil sunflower seeds, which birds prefer to the striped kind, attract titmice, chickadees, nuthatches, grosbeaks, towhees, jays, finches, cardinals, grackles, juncos, Carolina wrens, sparrows, woodpeckers, and blackbirds. Sunflower seed works well in tubular hanging feeders as well as hopper-style and platform feeders. White proso millet is a favorite of many ground-feeding species, including mourning doves, song-, white-crowned, and white-throated sparrows.

Seed mixes are also a good option for attracting birds. Be sure to check the contents of mixes you buy, because cheap ones often contain large quantities of inexpensive seeds that birds will ignore. Avoid a mix that contains a high percentage of buckwheat, cracked corn, golden or German millet, rape seed, or wheat, which are less attractive than other types of seed. Good seeds to look for in mixes include red proso millet, gray- or black-striped sunflower, and peanut hearts or kernels. Offer some seed on or near the ground to keep ground-feeders like sparrows, cardinals, jays, juncos, doves, northern bobwhites, and ring-necked pheasants happy.

Suet, the tallow-yielding fat around beef kidneys and loins, is high in calories and invaluable for helping birds keep warm in winter. While woodpeckers are especially dedicated visitors to suet feeders, many other birds also relish the treat. Chickadees, titmice, nuthatches, and several species of sparrows will all visit suet feeders. (You may even see flying squirrels balancing on your feeder at night.) Butchers and supermarkets sell suet, or you can buy it in cakes, rendered and rehardened with peanuts, seeds, and berries. Wire-mesh suet holders affix easily to trees or hang on metal stands with other bird feeders. Or simply hang chunks of suet in mesh bags.

USDA Plant Hardiness Zone Map

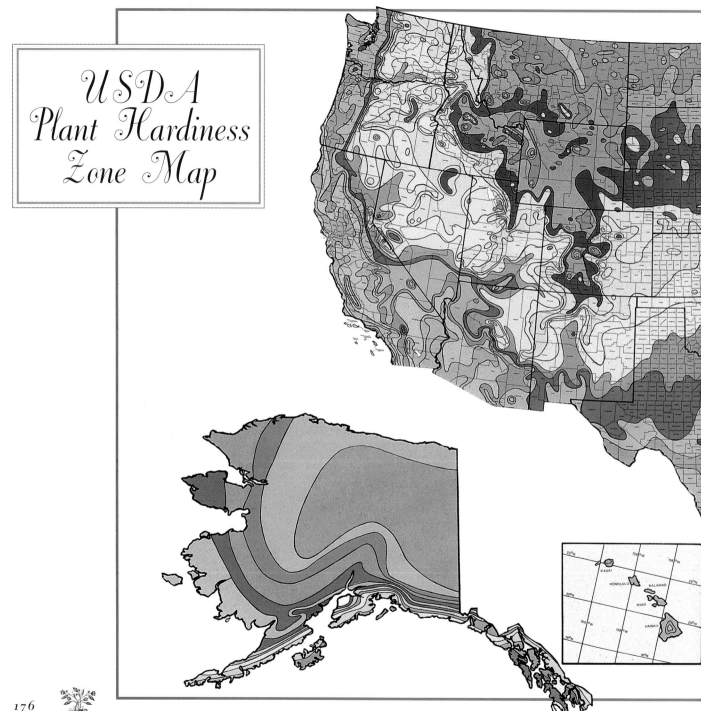

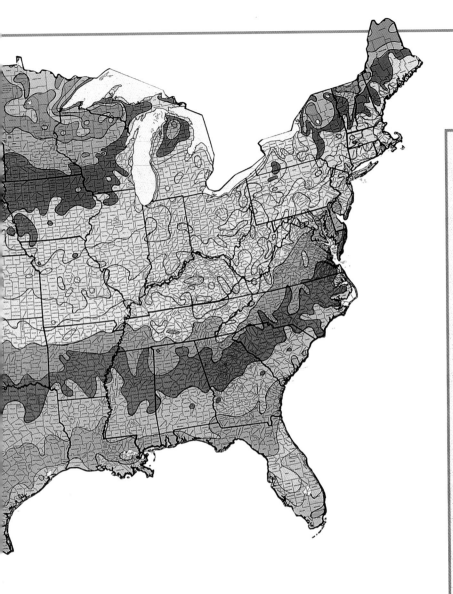

AVERAGE ANNUAL MINIMUM TEMPERATURE

Temperature (°C)	Zone	Temperature (°F)
-45.6 and Below	1	Below -50
-42.8 to -45.5	2a	-45 to -50
-40.0 to -42.7	2b	-40 to -45
-37.3 to -40.0	3a	-35 to -40
-34.5 to -37.2	3b	-30 to -35
-31.7 to -34.4	4a	-25 to -30
-28.9 to -31.6	4b	-20 to -25
-26.2 to -28.8	5a	-15 to -20
-23.4 to -26.1	5b	-10 to -15
-20.6 to -23.3	6a	-5 to -10
-17.8 to -20.5	6b	0 to -5
-15.0 to -17.7	7a	5 to 0
-12.3 to -15.0	7b	10 to 5
-9.5 to -12.2	8a	15 to 10
-6.7 to -9.4	8b	20 to 15
-3.9 to -6.6	9a	25 to 20
-1.2 to -3.8	9b	30 to 25
1.6 to -1.1	10a	35 to 30
4.4 to 1.7	10b	40 to 35
4.5 and Above	11	40 and Above

Resources

NURSERIES

Brent & Becky's Bulbs, Heath Enterprises, Ltd., 7463 Heath Trail, Gloucester, VA 23061; (804) 693-3966, fax: (804) 693-9436. Web site: www.brentandbeckysbulbs.com. Free catalogue. Specialize in bulbs.

W. Atlee Burpee & Co., 300 Park Ave., Warminster, PA 18974; (800) 888-1447. Web site: www.burpee.com. Free catalogue. Large variety of vegetable, flower, and herb seeds.

Busse Gardens, 5873 Oliver Ave. SW, Cokato, MN 55321-4229; (800) 544-3192, fax: (320) 286-6601. Catalogue, $2 (deductible from first order). Hostas, daylilies, peonies, Siberian iris, and perennials.

Carroll Gardens, 444 E. Main St., Westminster, MD 21157; (800) 638-6334, fax: (410) 857-4112. Catalogue, $3 (deductible from first order). Huge selection of perennials, herbs, vines, shrubs, and bulbs.

Collector's Nursery, 16804 N.E. 102nd Ave., Battle Ground, WA 98604; (360) 574-3832. Website:www.collectorsnursery.com. Catalogue, $2. Good source of interesting perennials.

Companion Plants, 7247 N. Coolville Ridge Rd., Athens, OH 45701; (740) 592-4643. Web site: www.frognet.net/companion_plants/. Large variety of herbs.

Dabney Herbs, P.O. Box 22061, Louisville, KY 40252; (502) 893-5198. Catalogue, $2. Specialize in herbs.

The Daffodil Mart, 30 Irene St., Torrington, CT 06790; (800) 255-2852. Free catalogue. Specialize in bulbs.

Fairweather Gardens, P.O. Box 330, Greenwich, NJ 08323; (609) 451-6261. Catalogue, $3. Great selection of trees and shrubs.

Fieldstone Gardens, Inc., 620 Quaker Lane, Vassalboro, ME 04989-9713; (207) 923-3836. Web site: www.fieldstonegardens.com. Catalogue, $2.50. Carry good amount of perennials and rock garden plants.

Forestfarm, 990 Tetherow Rd., Williams, OR 97544-9599; (541) 846-7269, fax: (541) 846-6963. Catalogue, $4. Western natives, perennials, trees, and shrubs.

Glasshouse Works, P.O. Box 97, Church St., Stewart, OH 45778-0097; (740) 662-2142, fax: (740) 662-2120. Web site: www.rareplants.com. Catalogue, $2. Great list of exotic and tropical plants.

Grigsby Cactus Gardens, 2354 Bella Vista Dr., Vista, CA 92084-7836; (760) 727-1323. Catalogue, $2 (deducted from first order). Good source for unusual cacti and succulents.

Harris Seeds, 60 Saginaw Dr., P.O. Box 22960, Rochester, NY 14692-2962; (800) 514-4441. Free catalogue. Vegetable and flower seeds.

Heronswood Nursery, Ltd., 7530 N.E. 288th St., Kingston, WA 98346; (360) 297-4172, fax: (360) 297-8321. Web site: www.heronswood.com. Catalogue, $8 (for a two-year subscription). Variety of perennials and woody plants.

Hydrangeas Plus, P.O. Box 389, Aurora, OR 97002; (503) 651-2887, fax: (503) 651-2648. Catalogue.

Jackson & Perkins Co., 2518 S. Pacific Hwy., Medford, OR 97501; (800) 292-4769, fax: (800) 242-0329. Web site: www.jacksonandperkins.com. Free catalogue. Roses.

Johnny's Selected Seeds, Foss Hill Rd., Albion, ME 04910-9731; (207) 437-4301, fax: (800) 437-4290. Web site: www.johnnyseeds.com. Free catalogue. Good source for annuals, herbs, and vegetables.

Klehm Nursery, 4210 N. Duncan Rd., Champaign, IL 61821; (800) 553-3715. Catalogue, $4. Peonies, hostas, daylilies, and iris.

Logee's Greenhouses, 141 North St., Danielson, CT 06239; (888) 330-8038, fax: (888) 774-9932. Web site: www.logees.com. Free catalogue. Begonias, rare plants, geraniums, and herbs.

McClure & Zimmerman, 108 W. Winnebago St., P.O. Box 368, Friesland, WI 53935; (800) 883-6998. Web site: www.mzbulb.com. Free catalogue. Bulbs.

The New Peony Farm, P.O. Box 18235, St. Paul, MN 55118; (651) 457-8994, fax: (651) 457-7635. Free catalogue.

Niche Gardens, 1111 Dawson Rd., Chapel Hill, NC 27516; (919) 967-0078. Web site: www.nichegdn.com. Catalogue, $3. Source of southwestern natives, ornamental grasses, shrubs, and more.

Nichols Garden Nursery, Inc., 1190 North Pacific Hwy., Albany, OR 97321; (541) 928-9280, fax: (541) 967-8406. Free catalogue. Herbs and vegetable seeds.

Ornamental Edibles, 3622 Weedin Ct., San Jose, CA 95132; (408) 946-7333, fax: (408) 946-0181. Catalogue, $2.

Park Seed Co., 1 Parkton Ave., Greenwood, SC 29647-0001; (800) 845-3369. Free catalogue. Flowers and vegetables.

Plant Delights Nursery, Inc., 9241 Sauls Rd., Raleigh, NC 27603; (919) 772-4794, fax: (919) 662-0370. Web site: www.plantdel.com. Catalogue. Wide variety of perennials, especially hostas.

Plants of the Southwest, Agua Fria, Rte. 6, Box 11A, Santa Fe, NM 87501; (800) 788-7333. Web site: www.plantsofthesouthwest.com. Catalogue, $3.50. Free price list. Southwestern wildflowers.

Richters Herbs, 357 Hwy. 47, Goodwood, Ontario, Canada L0C 1A0; (905) 640-6677, fax: (905) 640-6641. E-mail: inquiry@richters.com. Web site: www.richters.com. Free catalogue. Herbs.

Sandy Mush Herb Nursery, 316 Surrett Cove Rd., Leicester, NC 28748-5517; (828) 683-2014. Catalogue, $4. Herbs—seeds and plants.

Seeds of Change, P.O. Box 15700, Santa Fe, NM 87506-5700; (800) 95-SEEDS. Free catalogue. Huge selection of seeds.

Select Seeds–Antique Flowers, 180 Stickney Hill Rd., Union, CT 06076; (860) 684-9310, fax: (800) 653-3304. Web site: www.selectseeds.com. Catalogue, $1.

HEIRLOOM PERENNIALS

Shepherd's Garden Seeds, 30 Irene St., Torrington, CT 06790; (860) 482-3638. Web Site: www.shepherdseeds.com. Free catalogue. Great for the cooking gardener.

Stokes Seeds, Inc., P.O. Box 548, Buffalo, NY 14240-0548; (716) 695-6980. E-mail: Stokes@stokeseeds.com. Web site: www.stokeseeds.com. Free catalogue.

GREAT SELECTION OF VEGETABLES AND FLOWERS

Sunnybrook Farms, P.O. Box 6, 9448 Mayfield Rd., Chesterland, OH 44026; (440) 729-7232. Catalogue, $1. Herbs, scented geraniums, and hostas.

Thompson & Morgan, Inc., P.O. Box 1308, Jackson, NJ 08527-0308; (732) 363-2225. Free catalogue. Lots of seeds.

Van Bourgondien Bros., P.O. Box 1000, Babylon, NY 11702-9004; (800) 622-9997, fax: (516) 669-1228. E-mail: blooms@dutchbulbs.com. Free catalogue. Bulbs and perennials.

Wayside Gardens, 1 Garden Lane, Hodges SC 29695-0001; (800) 845-1124, fax: (800) 457-9712. Free catalogue. Ornamental trees and shrubs. Perennials and bulbs too.

White Flower Farm, P.O. Box 50, Litchfield, CT 06759-0050; (800) 503-9624. Web site: www.whiteflowerfarm.com. Free catalogue. Good general souce for perennials and shrubs.

Gilbert H. Wild & Son, P.O. Box 338, 3044 State Hwy. 37, Sarcoxie, MO 64862-0338; (888) 449-4537. Catalogue, $3. Peonies, daylilies, and iris.

SUNDRIES

Smith & Hawken, Two Arbor Lane, Box 6900, Florence KY 41022; (800) 776-3336.

Gardeners Eden, P.O. Box 7307, San Francisco, CA 94120; (800) 822-9600.

Gardener's Supply Co., 128 Intervale Rd., Burlington, VT 05401; (800) 688-5510. Web site: www.gardeners.com

Lee Valley Tools, P.O. Box 1780, Ogdensburg, N.Y. 13669; (800) 871-8158.

Glossary

Annual: A plant that germinates, blooms, sets seed, and dies, thus completing its entire life cycle in one growing season. Tender perennials are often treated as annuals in colder zones.

Biennial: A plant that completes its life cycle in two growing seasons. The first year it germinates and develops foliage. The plant overwinters, blossoms, sets seed, and dies the second season.

Bleed: Drip sap from a cut; especially refers to trees such as birch and maple.

Bolting: Rapid stem growth before flowering and seed set, often in response to stress.

Bud union: A swelling, also called the graft union, marking where a scion, or cut shoot, of a desired plant has been grafted onto sturdy rootstock.

Bulb: A horticultural term for underground storage organs, often used to include bulbs, corms, tubers, and thickened rhizomes. Botanically, a bulb is an underground storage organ composed of compressed leaves attached to a flat, stubby stem.

Corm: Compressed, enlarged stem that may be wrapped in last year's leaf bases. It grows below ground, stores food, and looks like a bulb.

Cultivar: Horticultural variety, usually increased by vegetative propagation, that may or may not come true from seed. Cultivar names follow a plant's botanical name and are set off by single quotes.

Deadhead: Cut off fading flowers to prevent seed formation, for neatness, and to encourage more blooms.

Force: Bring a plant or a cut stem of a plant into bloom ahead of its normal schedule.

Germination: Sprouting.

Half-hardy annual: Annual that tolerates very light frost.

Harden off: Gradually expose seedlings or houseplants raised indoors to outdoor growing conditions including sun, wind, heat, and cold.

Hardy annual: Plant such as sweet alyssum that can be direct seeded early, weathers frost, and blooms the same season.

Hardy perennial: Plant that tolerates differing degrees of cold weather. Check the USDA Plant Hardiness Zone Map (pages 176–77) to make sure that the perennials you choose will survive in your zone.

Hybrid: Cross between two or more parent plants.

Leaf scorch: Leaf damage caused by excess water loss through the leaves or inadequate water.

Mulch: Organic or inorganic material applied in a layer on garden soil to conserve moisture, smother weeds, and, if organic, improve soil texture. Mulches, including compost, shredded or decomposed leaves, shredded or chipped bark, buckwheat hulls, straw, and gravel, keep soil temperatures cooler in summer and warmer in winter.

Naturalization: Process of plants, especially non-native, escaping cultivation, growing wild, and multiplying freely in the landscape.

Perennial: Plant that survives for three or more growing seasons.

Pinch: Remove the growing tips of plants with the thumb and forefinger. Pinching encourages plants to grow bushier and more compact.

Species: The basic unit of plant classification; a group of plants with similar attributes that may breed among themselves.

Sucker: Shoot emerging from the root of a parent plant.

Transpiration: The process by which plants lose water through their leaves. Water loss increases when plants are exposed to high winds and when the weather is hot.

Truss: Dense cluster of flowers, as seen in rhododendron.

Tuberous root: Thick stem below ground used for food storage. Tubers bear buds, or eyes, from which new shoots and roots will develop.

Index

Note: Page numbers in **boldface** refer to illustrations.